Pam Weston was born in London in 1952. After an early child-hood illness, she experienced a loving, working-class childhood with her brother and parents. Pam married in 1972 and had a daughter in 1986. Following divorce two years later, Pam met her partner Keith and his two girls. They set up home and have been together ever since. Pam and Keith were both successful teachers before retiring. They now have four grandchildren, who keep them busy. This is Pam's first book inspired by events that took place between 2014 and 2019.

For my family
Albert Haynes – 1924–2014
Winifred Haynes – 1924–2017
Derek Haynes – 1949–2019
Keith, Ellie, Emma, Amy and my lovely grandchildren

Pam Weston

Mum, Me and Cancer

Austin Macauley Publishers™
LONDON • CAMBRIDGE • NEW YORK • SHARJAH

A CIP catalogue record for this title is available from the British Library.

ISBN 9781528950176 (Paperback)
ISBN 9781528950183 (Hardback)
ISBN 9781528972581 (ePub e-book)

www.austinmacauley.com

First Published (2020)
Austin Macauley Publishers Ltd
25 Canada Square
Canary Wharf
London
E14 5LQ

Thanks to everyone who encouraged me to write this book. Especially Juliet, who was my first reader.

Chapter 1
Goodnight, God Bless

When I heard the phone ring as I was showering at our B&B on the Isle of Wight, I knew. My partner, Keith, and I were on our annual pilgrimage to the scooter rally. It was Monday, August Bank Holiday in 2014 and we were up getting ready to catch the early ferry back. We had arrived on Friday with our friends. Keith had ridden across on the back of our friend Dave's 1960s scooter while Marie and I had driven over in the back-up car with our luggage and the emergency breakdown kit; 1960s scooters often break down! We set about having a good time.

Then on Saturday, my brother, Derek, had called from Lincolnshire to say that my dad had been admitted to hospital. This was not the first time this had happened. Dad, who was 90, had been in and out of hospital quite a bit in his long life but had always recovered. Derek reported that Mum had found him collapsed on the bedroom floor, the paramedics diagnosed him with pneumonia and he was on his way up to a ward. He had spent the day outside, clearing out weeds from his and his next-door neighbour's driveway, probably using a teaspoon to dig them out! That was the sort of person my dad was. Once he set his mind to a job, he wouldn't give up or ask for help. In other words, he was stubborn but lovely with it.

I guess Dad would have told those other patients all about his time in Norway, these stories were some of his favourites, he had loved his time there, never forgetting the kindness he had received. Dad had been sent to Norway after the Nazis had surrendered to decommission all of their vehicles. He had never been abroad so he found it exciting and very different. He was stationed just outside Oslo on a RAF camp which is where Oslo airport is now. He had never seen mountains except on his journeys to and from the Orkneys. He was amazed by the beauty of the fjords and the forests.

As a young man, he was curious about the place and its people. One day he decided to take a walk round a residential area, he saw a middle-aged woman sweeping her path and decided to try out his smattering of Norwegian, he said, "God Morgen," and so began a friendship between two families that would stretch across years. The woman spoke back but Dad couldn't understand her Norwegian and she spoke no English but she pointed to her watch to Dad and to her house and he guessed she was asking him to return a little later, he nodded. When he returned, he found the whole family there including a daughter who could speak English. The family were so grateful to be alive and free that they insisted on adopting Dad, he was made one of the family. I have photos of Dad dressed in the civilian clothes they gave him, a patterned jumper, corduroy trousers and a warm shirt. He topped this with his greatcoat.

As well as clothes they shared food with him. One Sunday he arrived early for lunch as instructed he went to fetch the meat, outside in the snow were several small sticks, when he pulled on one of the sticks a string came up and on the end was a piece of frozen meat which was placed in the oven. Dad said it was the best pork he had tasted until he was told it was whale! Each week he would visit and join in with the family and their friends, people would be invited specially to honour him.

Dad wanted to do something in return for this family who had been through hell and back. Their son, who had joined the resistance had had to flee to Sweden after his best friend had been shot jumping from his hiding place in the roof space of his family home. This family's son had come back but many hadn't. People had lived in fear, cowed by their circumstances, now they were coming alive again, picking up the pieces of their lives. Dad wanted to make a difference in some small way and his chance came quite quickly. On about his third visit the family had realised that he was a mechanic so he was taken into one of the outhouses, here covered in a blanket with lots of boxes piled on top, he found a hidden car. The family had kept it secret throughout the war so that it wouldn't be taken away and used by the enemy. They asked Dad if he could get it started. The rubbish and coverings were stripped off and Dad lifted the bonnet, he started laughing thinking they were playing a joke on him, there was no engine! Then the daughter took him to another outhouse and there scattered amongst several boxes he saw the engine all in pieces, the spark plugs in one, the starter motor in another, he then smiled it was just the sort of challenge he loved. Gradually after each of his visits the car was taking shape, one day the family gathered round while Dad started it, black smoke blew out of the exhaust but it was working. The family's first trip was with Dad to the Swedish border which they crossed for the first time for years, here they bought cigarettes and luxury goods not found in Norway, Dad told me everyone sang songs on the way back celebrating this new found freedom.

When he left Norway, Dad kept in touch with his Norwegian family. I loved it when the God Yul card would arrive addressed to us all. Somehow later they lost touch Dad really regretted this, then suddenly the grandson of the woman he had first met contacted Dad out of the blue, he had used the internet to find Dad and Mum and just turned up at their house. From then on, he visited Mum and Dad annually sharing stories his mother had told him and Dad would match these with his own. When my daughter visited Norway years later, she met younger members of the family who had all been told about a man called Bert who built a car from hundreds of pieces!

Later, my brother was able to reassure me that he was already improving and had told Derek that I mustn't rush up. This was typical of Dad, thinking about me and not wanting me to be driving all that way for no good reason. The next day, we heard that he was entertaining the staff and other patients with long-winded, funny stories! He told stories of how he grew up in London during the 20s, 30s and 40s. How as a young man he was always out to beat the system and make a bit of money alongside his younger brother, Bill. He spoke of his time in the RAF, especially the time he spent in Norway and then how he became a long-distance lorry driver first and then a London cabbie. He had a treasure trove of stories just right for every occasion, even when in hospital! As he got older, the stories got longer, as one inevitably led to another. Sometimes, we would have to hold the second course of a meal for up to 20 minutes while he caught up either with his story or with his eating! There was always just a little more that he needed to tell you.

Derek took Mum in to see him on Sunday and they hugged and when it came to the end of visiting, Derek promised to take her back, but that wasn't to be. During Sunday night, Dad's condition worsened and he died. Derek had waited until he thought we would be up to ring and tell me. It was devastating news and all I wanted to do was to get home to Mum. We drove to the ferry terminal, fittingly it was pouring. We queued in the car park for a place on the first ferry. When we were called forward, my car wouldn't start! I just burst into tears, but the ferry operators were unfazed and used jump leads to get me going, they became my heroes.

I dropped my friend off in Leicester and then drove on to Immingham through the torrential rain. I knew that I had to phone my daughter, Ellie, and was waiting to do so when she got home from work. She was living in Kent with her boyfriend, Ian, and I prayed that he would be there to comfort her. She would need comforting as Granddad was an absolute favourite. This was the man who had run behind her bike while she learnt to ride; the same man who had made her a doll's house and set it up with electric lighting; who carried her on his shoulders and who took her for weekends away in the caravan and loved her dearly. I pulled over at Tibshelf Services and phoned her. It was awful that she had no idea it was coming. I wanted to be with her, but I had to drive on. She promised me that she would phone Emma, Keith's eldest. I knew the girls would support each other. Although they were not related in blood to my dad and Mum, Emma and Amy had always been treated like grand-daughters, and in return they were very fond of Win and Bert.

I arrived in Lincolnshire at teatime; it was still raining. The house looked the same, but it couldn't be now. Mum heard my car and came into the kitchen to meet me. We hugged and cried together.

We had moved to Immingham when some new oil refin-eries were being built on the River Humber. Dad and Mum had always loved Yorkshire which you could see from the southern banks, it seemed a good opportunity to move closer to Mum's relatives. Dad had stopped driving taxis; traffic was getting worse in London and he had issues with what he called his nerves. The doctor had suggested driving around London during rush hours or doing continuous night work were not good for him. Dad found a job with a Petrol com-pany drivers, a tanker delivering outside London. Then the opportunity arose to transfer to Immingham. Only Dad had heard of the place, it was a small town with coal jetties out into the river. Its advantage was that there was a deep chan-nel in the river where large ships would pull in including petrochemical ships. It was forecast to become a 'boom town'. Dad applied for the move and it was agreed we would go in November 1966. My brother refused to come, he was eighteen, had a good job and a regular girlfriend. He loved living in London, on the scene. He refused. It must have been the worst time for Mum and Dad but they decided the opportunity was too good to miss, they also believed he would follow and they were right. He spent a few months living with his girlfriend's parents and when the romance died down, he joined us.

Dad had to go up first for a few weeks then he was of-fered a brand-new council house which he snapped up. We moved in when the plaster on the walls was still pink and wet. There were no street lights outside, one evening I fell down a large hole which had been dug during the day with no street lights I hadn't seen it. There was quite a big puddle in the bottom and I had to clamber up the slimy sides leaving a shoe behind. What a mess I looked when I arrived home. We quickly made friends with our neighbours and settled in. Next Dad went down to London to fetch his ageing parents up to live with us. Grandad had very bad bronchitis and needed to be somewhere where the air was cleaner, the council quickly found them a suitable flat. Then Auntie Flo arrived in the night with my cousins fleeing from her violent husband, they too were accommodated and then Mum's sister Kath moved over so that her husband and son could get jobs as Hull was in decline. Suddenly we had lots of our family around us again, the parties could begin.

We always loved family parties. When we were children, we had birthday parties that other kids were desperate to come to. Dad and a young, distant relative would dress up and do sketches, the most successful being a wallpapering skit where the younger man ended up pasted behind the wallpaper. Dad would wear a clown outfit and had us all in stitches. Then there would be the games, devised by Dad including his version of Double Your Money and Take Your Pick! Often us kids were tricked into thinking something was going to be easy then blindfolded and everything seemed so much harder. Dad did magic tricks and Mum provided the statutory buffet with sandwiches, jelly and of course cake.

Once the children's party was over the adults would prepare for the adult one. Us cousins were packed off to bed, often sleeping top to toe in a double bed where we talked for hours telling ghost stories and taking it in turn to creep out and see what the adults were up to. What we saw was dancing, drinking, Dad doing conjuring tricks and Auntie Flo finishing off the night by playing songs on her accordion that everyone knew and joined in with.

Dad had a particular party trick, the egg trick. For this he would line up glasses, up to 12 in a go but usually half a dozen. These glasses would be half full of water, then over them all he would place a metal tray with a cardboard roll taken from a cigarette packet on the tray over each glass then the raw egg balanced on top of each tube. After a countdown Dad would knock the tray out and the eggs would fall safely into the glasses unbroken. Unfortunately, at one party, Dad didn't hit the tray dead centre and twelve eggs hit the wall and slid down. No one seemed that bothered and Dad continued with his performances.

Once I arrived in Immingham time passed in a flurry of activity; my brother and I registered Dad's death and began letting people know. I walked everyday through the village, visiting the church where I had been married, the library where I had sometimes gone to study, the shops I knew so well and the sad little park where I hung out as a teenager. Sometimes I managed to encourage Mum to go with me but so many times someone would shout a "Hello" and follow it up by asking us where Dad was. I would have to step in and explain that Dad had died and that Mum was now on her own. I felt I had to protect her from having to say the word 'dead'. I went to the doctor's to let them know and the women behind the counter teared up and told me my dad was a 'gentleman'. I returned bags of medications to the local chemists who were rude and insensitive to me even though they knew the circumstances.

In the two weeks before the funeral, it became increasingly clear that Mum couldn't manage on her own, that Dad had taken over a lot of the chores. Although Dad was registered blind because of macular degeneration, he still had quite a lot of distance sight. So he often did the shopping as Mum had lost a lot of her mobility. When we did the washing, Mum couldn't hang out the washing as she was too unstable to stand and reach up, so Dad must have been doing that too. She also found it hard to bend down, so she couldn't reach low things. Even just getting from the sitting room to the kitchen seemed very hard for her sometimes, as she struggled out of the chair making little panting noises and occasionally gasping and moaning. Why hadn't I noticed this before? We visited regularly, but somehow when Dad was there these things must have been less obvious.

Between Dad dying and his funeral, I decided to clean the house ready for visitors. I found that the furniture hadn't been moved for a while. Wardrobes and drawers needed a good cleaning out, beds needed moving, and cupboards needed clearing. It was obvious that while Dad was doing the daily jobs, many things were deteriorating. Keith came up to stay for the middle weekend and we discussed what should happen. We agreed that as my brother spent five months of the year in Tenerife, we would have to convince Mum to live with us in Leicestershire. We would start by getting her to stay with us after the funeral. Keith went back to turn our second downstairs sitting room into a bed-sit for her. He ordered new furniture, moved ours into the garage and made it homely. I just had to make sure she came!

In fact, Mum showed that she was very aware that she couldn't stay in Lincolnshire even though deep down she wanted to. By the time the funeral arrived, it was all planned. Afterwards, Mum would go and stay with my brother and sister-in-law for a couple of nights while Keith and I went home to finish the preparations, and then Derek would drive her down to us and she would move in.

My family did us proud at the funeral, with cousins coming from London and Salisbury, plus my uncle Bill, Dad's younger brother, arriving with his wife, Jane. The Salisbury clan arrived in an old mini bus which they often used for family outings; they clambered out on to the drive. I had decided that we would all leave from Mum and Dad's small ex council house. I didn't want Mum to get to the crematorium and see everyone for the first time that day. I thought that might be too much for her, or was it that I might not cope? I knew I was keeping busy not giving myself time to think too much about Dad's death. Planning the funeral and the next steps engrossed me. I had been up early preparing breakfast baps for us all. My nephews arrived with their partners, our three girls with theirs plus our granddaughter, Lilli, who was just toddling. It was busy but comforting. Then the hearse arrived and the undertaker popped in to say we should be leaving. There was a rush to use the toilet and pop coats on. I asked Keith to see everyone out while I took Mum and got her in the car. We had only ordered one car to follow as all the girls wanted to go in their own. Keith locked up the house and we left in a convoy with everyone following the lead car into Grimsby, which was nine miles away.

We arrived at the Crem to find more family and friends waiting for us. I had decided to speak at the funeral and was nervous about whether I would manage it. I had a speech about my dad and his adventures in my pocket which I kept touching. I also had a letter that I wanted to leave on the coffin. There were roses from Mum, the girls and I plus Keith left a small section of a map of Scotland; this alluded to a story Dad had told frequently.

When Dad was sent over to Norway at the end of the war to decommission German vehicles, he left from a dock somewhere in Scotland. He had no idea where, he just knew that he had been driven down from the Orkneys and had to wait three days on the dockside. As it was wartime, there were no signposts and no clues except that Dad had stayed on a RAF camp for one night. Dad knew it was close to the Firth of Forth as he remembered the bridge. Every time he told this story, which was many, he bemoaned the fact that he didn't know where he had left from; he would always then go on to tell us how, during the night on the ship, he woke up as the engines had stopped. Being curious, he went up on the deck to find they were in the middle of a minefield and the sailors were hanging over the sides with what looked like broom handles pushing the mines away from the sides of the boat! Dad was told to get back down below decks quickly and stay there. The next day, they arrived safely in Norway. One evening, Keith sat with Dad and a laptop for several hours piecing together the things Dad did know and managed to prove, with the help of maps and old photos, that the port must have been Roslaire. Keith left a fragment of a large map of Scotland on Dad's coffin showing the location for his Norway departure. My daughter, Ellie, had also written a letter, no doubt, remembering the childhood fun and trips in Nanny and Granddad's caravan.

As we got out of the car, I became aware that Ellie and her boyfriend, Ian, were missing. Emma was on her mobile, giving them directions; they had been left behind and were going to be late. The undertaker was calling us forward. We had to go in, otherwise we would miss our allocated time. I started to panic; we couldn't have the funeral without her, but we couldn't delay. Our humanist leader started the service and I knew I was to speak next. What could I do? As he handed over to me, I saw her run in at the back and throw herself in a seat next to Emma. Suddenly, I found the strength to stand up and pay tribute to my fantastic Dad. Afterwards, I found out that poor Ian had been last in the queue for the toilet and Keith had thought everyone had left, so he locked the house up. Ellie had been waiting in her car when the cortege left with everyone else following. She had gone back to find Ian shouting through the letterbox! She had no keys but luckily remembered that Granddad kept the keys to the conservatory in a mug. She directed Ian to them, he escaped into the back garden, then jumped over next door's wall to get to the street as Dad had secured his garden with locked side doors and high fencing long ago. Dad was always security conscious, good job that our neighbours weren't as bothered.

After the service, we all placed our gifts on the coffin. I watched as my brother helped my mum across. She placed the rose on the coffin, then kissed her fingers and touched the wood. At the door, she turned and blew a gentle kiss before stepping outside. I was to see this gesture of blowing a kiss many more times, and it is how I think of her often.

At the 'Do' after, my auntie, Dot, sat with Mum and comforted her, no doubt talking about trips to Yorkshire and holidays they'd had together in and around Scarborough. I circulated thanking people for coming. Loads of friends and relatives had stories to tell about how Dad had helped them with something or given good advice. My London cousins remembered my dad going down to fetch them and their mum, his sister, to live with us when her marriage fell apart. Dad had finished work then driven down from Lincolnshire to pick them up with the few belongings they had taken from the marital home. My cousin from my mum's side of the family talked about how his father and mother had moved over from Yorkshire to Lincolnshire to take up jobs in the new petrochemical industry that Dad had heard about which he thought might suit them. Again, he helped them move into the new council houses that were on offer for those like him, willing to relocate. Immingham was almost a 'new town', then with houses going up every day. Some of Mum and Dad's original neighbours attended the funeral, saying that Dad was always willing to give anyone a hand.

After the buffet, people started to drift off. Derek took Mum back to her house for what was going to be the last time she slept in it. I walked back with Keith, glad to have a few minutes to think about what people had said, and to store it in my memory. When we got back, Ellie had fetched some old photos down; she and Mum were looking through them. Mum was naming the faces and Ellie was asking questions. I thought that Dad would have loved to have been there to tell a few stories associated with those photos. We didn't stay up late; we were tired. Ellie put the photos in the cupboard in my old box room where she was sleeping. In the middle of the night, I woke up with a start; there had been a loud noise of some sort. I ran out onto the landing and bumped into Ellie who looked as white as a ghost. The photos had hurled themselves off the shelf and out of the cupboard onto the floor by Ellie's bed. "Do you think it was Granddad?" Ellie whispered.

"No," I replied, "He would never frighten us. You didn't put them away properly." I'm not sure she was convinced or was it me who needed convincing?

Chapter 2
Home from Home

We shouldn't have been surprised that the death of my dad and the move from the family home would be traumatic for my mum, given that they had been married for 69 years and had lived in the house in Lincolnshire for over 40 years.

They had met during the war when Dad's RAF squadron was stationed at Patrington in Yorkshire. This was an isolated spot, very close to Spurn Point. Mum was a Yorkshire lass from Hull who was doing her bit for the war effort, working on a farm as part of the Women's Land Army. Mum was seeing a young man known as Ginge from the RAF and he asked her to line up a friend for a blind date with his friend, Bert, and one evening they met up. They did one of the few things available to courting couples during the war; they went to the pictures together in Withernsea. Dad could always get hold of transport as he was a driver/mechanic. During the evening, Dad decided that he was far more interested in Mum than his blind date. Mum was shy but funny and quite feisty. Mum was also having second thoughts about her date as she compared him to the young, blue-eyed, blond cockney he'd brought with him. Both honourably stuck with their date for the evening, but Dad found out later that week that Mum had broken off with Ginge and was now available. The only problem was that he couldn't really ask his mate for her details, so instead he took every opportunity he had to go out in a vehicle and drive around the countryside peering into the fields and farms. Eventually, he spotted Mum in her Jodhpur-like trousers and fair-isle sweater, with a headscarf tied around her dark curls. He stopped, they talked and the rest, as they say, is history.

Dad had been seeing someone at home; Hilda was an East End girl from a large family that Dad loved being part of. He had to tell her he had met someone else and he was dreading it. He wrote to her as soon as he could, a difficult letter, but Dad did the right thing. Mum and Dad were married on 22 April 1945 in Hull. The wedding dress was long, lacy and shared with about ten other brides that year! Dad's family made it up to Yorkshire. In the photo, Dad is smiling broadly, wearing his RAF uniform with pride, and his sister, Flo, is wearing a smart suit that she tailored herself. Bill, his younger brother, is in civvies while my granddad grins out, no doubt glad to be away from the army for a while, having been in Europe for most of the war. My nanny is wearing a utility suit with a jaunty little hat; I bet she thought she was the bee's knees up from London! Dad found out later that had they all walked a couple of streets away, they would have come across another wedding taking place at almost the same time at the Catholic Church. It was his old girlfriend, Hilda, marrying Pete, a Yorkshireman from Hull whom she had met in London! What a strange coincidence; the couples were to reunite after the war and the two couples became good friends for life.

Dad loved Yorkshire and he loved Mum's family. Her father, who was a night watchman, was tall, slim, quietly spoken, and above all, kind. His wife was shorter and rounder and had a soft, cuddly look. They welcomed this slightly cocky Londoner that their Winnie brought into their home, sharing rations with him while he provided chocolate for the parents and stockings for the three girls. Mum had two older sisters. Edna, the eldest, was already married but still went out dancing and enjoyed flirting. Kath was younger and had an infectious laugh. They always had fun when they were all together. The eldest child of the family was Lenny who was in the army somewhere, so they saw very little of him. He, too, was already married with children. The baby of the family was Harold who was my mum's favourite, and he also

21

became my dad's favourite. After the war, Harold met and married Dot, a girl from the West Midlands and together with Mum and Dad, they spent many wonderful days exploring Yorkshire. When Mum had moved down to London, she had left behind everything familiar to her but it was Dad who longed to be in Yorkshire. Mum loved visiting her family and sometimes Mum, Derek and I would go on the steam train to Hull and stay at Mum's sister Kath's house. This was a massive adventure. We always had fun, we would eat fish patties and chips, pikelets, baps and fat rascals, all things not seen or heard of in London. Our cousins were slightly older than us, they took us fishing in the local cut and we played hide and seek in the grinnell's. Sometimes Dad would borrow or buy a cheap car and we would squeeze in and drive up to Yorkshire stopping at transport cafes on the way where we ate hearty, fried food and drank thick tea from pint mugs. Once in Yorkshire we always visited the seaside. Two or three times we stayed at Primrose Valley, a large caravan site near Withernsea. The caravans had no toilets or wash facilities, these were located in wooden huts dotted about the fields. Dad also liked the moors so we would all squeeze back into the car for a drive round. I can't remember us doing much, it was a cheap holiday and we loved it!

Often, I would wonder if Mum was thinking of the old days when she sat silent on our settee hardly saying or doing anything. Did she think about that first date? We didn't know what was going on in her head.; Like many of her generation who had been through World War 2, Mum was a stoic. It was difficult to know what she was thinking or feeling, as her 'stiff upper lip' got in the way. She would get up mid-morning, eat breakfast and then make her way to the front room where she would stay until bedtime. Keith had set up our back-sitting room as a bed-sit for Mum with new furniture, a TV and comfortable chair, but she hardly ever used it except for sleeping.

This bed-sitting room was a temporary measure until we could find Mum somewhere to live where she could be more independent. Luckily for us, a brand-new sheltered complex was being built on the edge of our village. It was to have 50 flats and ten bungalows. Inside the main building would be a communal lounge, dining room, hairdressers, craft room and cinema, as well as a little shop. The most important element was that it would have 24/7 staffing and that would mean peace of mind for us. It was due to be finished in April, just 7 months away. That would give us time to convince Mum that she should sell her house to live near us permanently.

In the first few weeks that Mum lived with us, she would suddenly say something like, "I can't understand why X didn't come to the funeral." We would explain that, in fact, X had been at the funeral and had spoken to Mum, or that we'd had a card from X explaining why they weren't there. Sometimes, she would repeat the same comment a few days later and we would patiently explain again. It became obvious to us that she was trying to process what had happened to her. We were sympathetic but as the time went on, it became harder to live with Mum. Suddenly, we felt tied to the house; we had to plan our days so that one of us was there at lunch to check if Mum was eating. Otherwise, she would just go without. If we went out together, we had to rush back as we could feel that Mum was unhappy about being left. We had always danced most Saturday nights and sometimes twice a weekend, but now we felt guilty if we did that. Sometimes Keith would go on his own with our friends and I would stay behind, not being able to face telling Mum we were leaving her alone.

Keith and I have three daughters between us. Emma, Keith's eldest, lives in Bristol with her husband, Stan; Amy is Keith's youngest and she lives with her husband, Andy; and Lilli, our first grandchild, about three miles away. My daughter is Eleanor or Ellie. At this time she was living in Deal in Kent and working at the South Foreland Lighthouse, a National Trust property, on the top of the White Cliffs of Dover. Amy lived locally but had a toddler to care for, while the other two lived further away. This meant that it was impossible to ask them to 'Mum sit'. My brother and his wife split their time between living in Lincolnshire and Tenerife.

Mum knew nobody in the village, so we were her lifeline and we were beginning to feel the strain.

Mum wouldn't talk about Dad. If I tried to start a conversation about the past, she would close it down with a quick 'Yes' or 'No', then nothing. I know that during this period I probably made things worse by molly coddling her. I would watch her trying to second-guess what she might want. I was always putting the kettle on for a drink, buying her cakes and treats, and cooking meals with her in mind. At night, I would put out her breakfast bowl and cereal just as my dad had done for years, so that all Mum had to do was switch on the already boiled kettle! Food was always important to Mum and Dad; again, I think this was a throwback to a poor childhood and the war when they would eat whatever was available, as they never knew when they would get the next meal. The highlight of any day out was eating. Mum particularly loved ice cream and cakes, but Dad loved a hearty meal of fish and chips, with tea plus bread and butter and a mug of strong tea.

Talking of ice cream reminds me of travelling to Scarborough with Mum, Dad, Auntie Dot and Uncle Harold. Dad would drive and I would be squashed in the back between Dot and Mum; my parents would be smoking, so it wasn't pleasant! I would try and catch a glimpse of the countryside through the blue mist and eventually we would pull into Scarborough. Mum, Dot and I would be dropped off right down by the fishing boats while Harold and Dad went to park the car. No time would be wasted to get to the ice cream parlour where the adults would tuck into a Knickerbocker glory made with fruit salad, ice cream, jelly and a little squirty cream. This was a family ritual; the parlour is still there even though many of its customers are long gone. After a visit to Scarborough when I was in my teens, Mum noticed that the shops were now stocking squirty cream in aerosol cans so she bought some and used it on puddings once. Then it got lost in the back of the fridge until I turned up with a boyfriend in tow. Mum wanted to impress, so she had bought lemon meringue and then produced the squirty cream and there in front of my boyfriend, she squirted a flourish across his pie; the cream was totally green! Needless to say, we didn't eat it apart from Dad who couldn't stand waste. He scraped off the green cream and ate the lot with no repercussions.

Back in Leicester, the only time that Mum really came alive was once a week on a Tuesday when our granddaughter came to stay. As a one-year-old, Lilli was delightful, lively and inquisitive. Lilli would lie on the floor and Mum would sit on the settee leaning over to make her giggle. Suddenly Mum was talking to Lilli, laughing with her, and making noises, even gurning! We would hear her thoughts about child rearing. Suddenly on Tuesdays it felt like she had a reason to be. Mum had three great-grandchildren at this point; Emily, Thomas and Lilli. Emily and Thomas were older and lived in Hitchin. They were the children of my brother's oldest son, Steven, and his lovely wife, Jess. Mum spoke about her great-grandchildren often. Steven would send photos to my iPad to show Mum. Many times I blessed him for these as they gave Mum and me something to talk about. We would check out Thomas' hairstyles, be amazed at Emily's long legs and keep up-to-date with family outings. We saw them camping, toasting marshmallows, crabbing on the beach and fishing in rock pools. The little videos we received were always exciting, with Thomas playing football, Emily dancing. We lived their lives vicariously. When they visited, it was as if royalty were arriving. Everything had to be just right; the food had to be suitable, there had to be little gifts and things to play with. The anticipation of a visit was almost as good as the visit itself. Then after they had gone, Mum would spend days thinking back and mentioning the things she'd noticed and the things the kids had said. Precious times!

Mum and Dad had been members of the Caravan Club for years and they travelled all over the UK with their trusty caravan. Everywhere they went, they would bring back presents for first their grandchildren, then their great-grandchildren. Sometimes they were pretty straightforward, like purses for the girls, always containing a coin for good luck and pens for the boys, but sometimes the presents were more off the wall. Two that I particularly remember are a hula-hula doll that danced on a stand moving her hips from side to side to the tune of the Macarena! This came from a wonderful shop called Yubba Dubba Doos found on the Lincolnshire coast. As I write, I know that this doll, given to my daughter when she was about 10, is still in our shed even though my daughter is now over 30! A more recent purchase is the monkey Mum bought for Lilli when she was two. I decided to get Mum the Argos catalogue in the run up to Christmas, what a wonderful find it was. Mum spent hours poring over it, choosing her presents for others. We would spend hours choosing between one thing and another over a cup of tea, then all I had to do was order and collect. So Mum ordered a laughing monkey; when it came, not only did it laugh, but it farted very loudly, Lilli loved it and two years later, still does. We adults hide it frequently but Lilli digs it out again. Mum had a way of knowing just what would please the children and surprise the adults.

Time passed, but often very slowly and quite painfully in our amalgamated household. When we could, Keith and I would escape for a walk around the village and a coffee at the local pub. We would always walk past the supported living complex Oak Court at least once a week to see how the build was progressing. Then we would steal a few minutes for ourselves by sitting in the local pub's garden drinking our coffee and eating a mini brownie with one eye on the time, heaven! Keith and I didn't have time to consider each other, we just had to get on with living day by day. I realised later that by immersing myself in looking after Mum, I didn't give myself a chance to grieve for Dad. This all came crashing down about my ears one night when we had escaped with friends for a few hours. We were at one of our regular haunts full of people we knew, I can't even remember what triggered it, but suddenly I felt an enormous tsunami of grief rush across the dancefloor and envelope me. I sat absolutely still; I knew that if I moved or spoke, I would release all my grief. A friend came over, touched my shoulder and I immediately burst into tears, ran from the room and locked myself in the ladies' room to cry and cry until I was empty and exhausted. Tears and snot ran down my face but I didn't care. Keith and my friends rescued me and took me home, I could feel the love and concern in the car as we drove fast down the M1 back to Leicester. I could feel their love but I couldn't respond – I had nothing left for them.

Ellie and I had recently taken a pilgrimage to the Orkneys where Dad had been stationed as a young member of the RAF. He had joined up as soon as the war started. Of course, as a 16-year-old he had wanted to fly planes and attended a selection centre in London where he had to take a test. Having left school at 14 he wasn't the greatest reader and he found the test difficult full of maths problems, number strung together with words. Once he'd finished the test he was interviewed and it was obvious he wasn't fighter pilot material, instead he was offered a driver / mechanic post. He accepted. As a young man Dad had always been interested in how things work especially the new combustion engine. Dad told a story about a school lesson when all the boys were being shown an engine stripped down and on display. The teacher started to tell them how it worked then got called over to the door by another colleague. After a few moments the boys were getting restless so Dad took over explaining how everything worked pointing out the spark plugs and the carburettor. He got carried away and when he finished the teacher, who had returned a few minutes earlier applauded his efforts!

While still at school Dad took every opportunity to look at and work on cars and even to drive them. My Grandad was a driver for a rich fish merchant. He drove the man and his wife around London on errands and social visits. The car was kept in a garage and Grandad and Nanny lived in a small flat over the top. At weekends Grandad washed and cleaned the car ready for the next week. When he reversed it out of the garage, all the kids from the street would come to look at it. Sometimes his boss let Grandad take the car and use it to take the family out. Once when Dad was just 12 the family went down to Kent, for a weekend, to visit an aunt who had taken her family down to hop pick. They were staying in a camp full of Londoners. Grandad let Dad drive the car along the quiet Kent roads but unfortunately, they happened to drive past a local police officer who tracked them down to the Londoner's camp and charged Grandad with allowing a minor to drive, it looked like Grandad would lose his licence and his job. The incident was reported in the local paper and a London paper picked it up, this meant Grandad's boss and neighbours found out what was going on. Grandad was called in to see the fishmonger and expected the worst to happen, what would he do without his livelihood, times were hard for many. In fact his boss had called him in to say he was writing a letter in support of Grandad's good character and would be asking others to do likewise. When Grandad appeared in court, he got away with just a warning. So Dad was probably always destined, from an early age to be a driver/mechanic.

Dad took up his RAF posting and was trained at Skegness, marching on the car park of The Ship pub. Once trained he was posted to the Orkneys. He didn't like it much as it was as far away from London as it could be both in terms of the physical distance and the type of place. Dad was used to the hubbub of the city and here he was on a series of small islands north of the country. He especially didn't like the rough crossing which Ellie and I experienced on our short visit. It is one of the roughest areas of water surrounding Britain as several different currents meet to make it choppy. We had flown up to Inverness and then taken a coach through beautiful countryside to the coast, we arrived at Scrabster on a cold, February evening and watched our ferry pull in. Once loaded it set off for Stromness. Almost as soon as we left the dock the ship started rolling! I remembered my dad telling me that as soon as he got to the dock, he would make his way up onto the deck and find a quiet spot. He would lie down with his kit bag under his head and wrap himself in his grey RAF greatcoat and fall asleep and hope to sleep for the whole crossing otherwise he would be seasick. Ellie and I didn't sleep but we found ourselves up on deck gripping the rail trying to keep our eyes steady with a moving horizon. We made it without being sick but only just. We felt very close to Dad.

While on the Orkneys we visited the camp where Dad had spent many months, the buildings have nearly all gone except for the NAAFI and the gate, which would have been guarded. As we gazed out across the desolate view in the pouring rain I thought of Dad, just a young boy, trying to keep himself busy. He had told me that he walked a lot and he stumbled across an archaeological site which he thought was Roman. He had described it to me how it nestled next to the sea and how amazed he was to walk amongst the 'rooms'. In fact this was Skara Brae, a Neolithic site of immense importance. Ellie and I walked in my dad's steps, well almost as visitors are not allowed to walk in the 'rooms' nowadays but we stood above the settlement and looked down in to it and out to sea as he had done all those years before.

I had never really thought about why my dad was posted to the Orkneys but while there I found a book about life during the war and everything became clear, the RAF were on Orkney to protect allied shipping and submarines who often moored on Scapa Flow. In the book there was an excerpt from the log of the RAF station, I was amazed to find that almost every night during the period recorded there was some alert, sometimes planes were scrambled sometimes the camp was just put on alert. Dad may have found the days pretty boring but the nights must have been busy. During those boring days Dad also played tricks on his fellow air men. A new colleague had arrived from down south. He noticed that at night there were sometimes flashing lights in the sky and so he asked Dad what it was. Dad told him that it was a trolley bus that ran from one island to the other late at night picking up revellers, the man decided to take a ride and set off one evening to find the trolley stop, of course it was the Northern Lights he was chasing. Ellie and I didn't see the

Northern Lights as it rained in sheets while we were there but we did catch a glimpse of my young Dad going about his business.

Time was passing, things were not getting easier; in fact, they were getting harder. We expected Mum to stay until April, but she eventually stayed with us for 16 months in total. I loved Mum but there were habits I found so difficult. Mum never considered going to watch TV in her room so we were under scrutiny all the time. We felt watched and somehow judged as falling short in our endeavours. There was something about Mum's gaze that seemed critical.

In January 2015, Mum was ill, she looked pale and was lethargic. The GP came, took blood tests and checked Mum over. The next day she rang to ask to come and see me and then Mum – this wasn't going to be good news. She told me that Mum had a low blood count, probably because she was bleeding internally. This was likely to be the return of her bowel cancer. Mum had been diagnosed with bowel cancer when she was 86 and had an operation where they removed part of her bowel. This had been very successful; in fact, Mum was so well afterwards that she seemed about ten years younger for a while. We always knew that there was a chance it would return, just our luck that it looked like now was that moment. The doctor told me that Mum should go to the hospital but I knew that was the last thing Mum would want.

Mum hated hospitals and was always badly behaved when in one. Dad was always quite happy to be in hospital, he felt it was the right place to be if you were ill. He trusted the nurses and doctors and co-operated with every treatment. He would make jokes to keep everyone amused – the staff always loved him. Not so with Mum; she would be awkward and uncooperative, demand to go home, and even refuse to eat the food. I explained this to the very young doctor and asked if it was really necessary for her to go in. I could see she was hesitating, so I personalised it by asking her if it was her grandma, would she recommend hospital. I knew that Mum would not want further surgery, so I believed that she could get good care at home without the risk of infection. The doctor agreed. We told Mum together what we thought was going on in her body. Mum had never been good at biology; she didn't understand how her body worked but she understood what we were saying. The doctor told her that her body might start to shut down, in this instance did she want resuscitating? Mum said, "No, I've had my life." It was a devastating moment, but I had read about the elderly being resuscitated and didn't want Mum to go through that, so I was sad but relieved.

After I had seen the doctor out, I settled Mum down with a cup of tea and a biscuit and got myself a coffee. I realised with horror that I had not involved Keith in this momentous decision. I was going to have to tell him that I had promised Mum that she could stay in our back room and possibly die there. He took it well, just making me promise him that each and every morning I would go in first and check on Mum, check that she was still alive. That is exactly what I did and every day she was. In some ways I wasn't at all surprised as we always said that Mum was 'a tough old bird' and that she could live to be 100. Each day she seemed to improve and her rising blood count confirmed this – she was on the mend again.

Chapter 3
Bad Habits

At Xmas we got together as a family, 14 of us! It was a bit hollow, when I look at the photos, I see Mum and me wearing funny hats, smiling just for the camera. I felt very tired and I guess Mum felt the same. Keith and I were looking forward to a break in Tenerife while my brother was back in this country, but this wasn't to be. Just after Christmas Mum became ill with a bad cold that turned into a nasty chest infection. My brother was due to collect Mum for the week but she really wasn't up to going. I had to admit that I was scared to leave her in case it got worse, Keith understood and we cancelled. We spent the first part of the New Year trying to get some money back, something we were to do again and again in the future. We couldn't help but be sad about not going away, but we tried not to let our disappointment show, after all it wasn't Mum's fault.

No one should think that we didn't love my mother – we did. However, we found some of her habits difficult to bear. Most embarrassing was that sometimes she didn't smell good because she leaked urine. Sitting on our settee all day trying to avoid getting up and making the arduous trip to the loo didn't help. Mum would always leave it to the last minute, as it was hard work for her to get to the loo because of the set-up of our house. She had to walk through the dining room and kitchen to the downstairs shower room. Mum also refused to use our shower. Soon after she moved in, we had a man come out from social care to put in a handle and we had a seat in the shower tray, but she still refused to shower regularly, preferring an 'all over wash'! I think she found it difficult to manoeuvre in the small shower cubicle. Each night after she had gone to bed, we sprayed the settee with cleaning foam and placed the seat against the radiator to dry for the next day. Mum never knew we did it, out of love I couldn't raise the subject with her.

She also began wearing the same clothes every day, even though she had a wardrobe full. I had to start going into her room when she was asleep in the morning and grabbing clothes to put in the wash, otherwise she would wear the same pair of trousers all week. Keith and I particularly hated a pair of checked trousers that were totally worn out. One day, Keith lost his cool and I found him ripping them before putting them in the washer. When they came out, he explained to Mum that they must have got caught in the drum and were beyond saving. We treated Mum to a new pair! Wearing the same clothes continually was hard to square with the mother I remembered as a young woman. Although we didn't have loads of money, Mum had always been interested in fashion. When I was 13 in 1965, she made herself a new style shift dress. She used a simple pattern, cutting it out on the sitting room floor and sewing it on her old Singer sewing machine. It was flame coloured. She had overestimated the material and the next morning draped across my bed was a smaller version. We loved those dresses and wore them together often. I still have Mum's mock Astrakhan coat, bought in the early 60s and worn for nights out. I have worn it on New Year's Eve just as she used to and felt glamorous. Now she didn't seem to care what she looked like.

Mum also developed a habit of not always eating with her knife and fork. We always ate at our dining room table together. More and more, we found Mum picking up her food. She had a bit of a claw-like finger which was the result of chopping off the end of it in a turnip-cutting machine while in the land army. The farmer had held the finger together whilst driving a tractor one-handed to have it stitched. He saved the finger but whoever stitched it back together did a poor job resulting in a crooked-looking thing. Mum would reach out suddenly with this finger and hook things off the plate. How can you tell your mother to behave? I couldn't. It was only later that I realised that Mum's arthritis was probably the cause of this bad habit. I noticed that often when she held her knife or fork, her hand would lock into a set position and she would then need to peel her fingers off the implement so using her fingers was probably easier and less painful. Mum also had to give up knitting and sewing for the same reason which was a real sadness to her. Mum knitted loads of things for me when I was young, but not always successfully. Once when I was at college, she knitted me a massively over-sized jumper with a big roll collar – just what I had asked for. Believe it or not, this was what trendy students were wearing in the 1970s! I tried it on, or I should say I tried to get it on, but found that the neck part was so small I couldn't actually get it over my head! I struggled with it and got it halfway, then couldn't get it on or off. By the time my friends released me, I had a red line across my forehead that stayed with me for hours.

Another annoying habit of Mum's was that she used, what seemed like, millions of tissues. We would find them tucked down the cushions of the settee, on the coffee table, in her bed, on the kitchen surfaces; in fact, there would be a trail wherever Mum had been. Most annoying of all was that we would find them in the washing after it had been through the washer. The number of rolls of Sellotape we used taking off flecks of tissue probably kept a whole factory going and could have secured our Christmas presents for the next ten years! Even after we checked all pockets, we would be caught out because Mum would tuck tissues up her sleeves, in her bras and even in her socks – we could never win.

Trumping was another problem. We have a small sitting room and sometimes it was unbearable. We tried to work out what it was that I was cooking that caused such flatulence but we couldn't find the solution. I had adjusted my cooking for Mum as she didn't like spicy food, so our favourite chilli was off the menu, as was any form of curry, but still the problem persisted. I started cutting out different foodstuffs each week but never found the culprit. Mum could win a contest with the farting monkey hands down!

Our main concern with Mum was her lack of an opinion. If I asked her what she would like to eat, she would just say, "What do you fancy? I'll have anything." This sounds great to cater for someone who isn't picky but we found it really hard not knowing how she was feeling. If we offered to take her out, she would always say something like, "It's up to you. If you want, we can go. I don't mind." What did that mean? Did she want to go, or was she agreeing to please us? We needed some clues or just some straight answers, but we hardly got any.

Then there were the silences. Keith was much better at these; he could read or be looking at the internet. I felt as if I had to draw her into things I was doing. I started doing jig-saws because they had been one of Mum's favourite things. I would sit with the board, sorting out the straight bits, en-couraging her to join in, but she wasn't really bothered; it was as if she only did it to please me.

Mum had always been an avid reader. When I was young, I borrowed and read all her Jean Plaidy historical novels. They gave me a good grounding in some periods of history. It was Mum's reading habits and Dad taking me to see statues and historical buildings in and around London that made me want to study history at college. There are many charity shops in our village with an endless supply of second – hand books, so I would choose some titles for Mum but she would read a bit, place the book on the side somewhere (usually next to a tissue) and declare that it wasn't much good. There it would stay until I took it back and the whole process was repeated.

Keith and I would talk in bed about how we felt. We were tired – well, more like exhausted, demoralised and there was no end in sight. We felt disloyal and petty. We ra-tionalised that Mum was grieving Dad and her loss of the house and independence and sometimes that made us feel better, but often we understood why she was like she was; it didn't help us to cope on a daily basis at all.

We tried to do things to take Mum out of herself to get her interested in life, some of these were pretty successful, others were not.

As children Dad and Mum had taken us on many outings. Our family favourite was probably Runnymede. On any sunny day in the summer, you would find us there with our cousins Elaine and Rosie and their parents Flo, my dad's elder sister and her husband Stan. I have photos of us all sitting on blankets on the floor tucking in to a picnic together. Mum had a picnic set that came in a small, flat suitcase. I loved that set especially the little spoons and the plastic egg cups, which we never actually used. Mum would pack sandwiches for everyone along with cucumber chunks, tomatoes and hard-boiled eggs which would be eaten with a pinch of salt. There would also be squashed swiss roll and our all-time favourite Battenberg cake! Dad would set up the small primus stove and brew some tea.

Runnymede is well known now as being the place where the Magna Carta was signed but for us it was just a field at the side of the River Thames. In the 50s and 60s those with cars took them everywhere and ours was always parked as close to the river as possible. Dad would bring inner tubes from out of lorry tyres and use a pump to blow these up. Then with all us kids safely wrapped in our tubes we would swim in the river. We had to stay near the side to avoid some of the pleasure boats passing by but generally the river was quieter then. After a good swim we would run around and play three catches and out until we were dry. After lunch a party would usually set off across the road and up the hill on the other side. We would walk through the woods picking flowers as we went, it was wonderful when the bluebells were out the whole floor was carpeted in purply blue. When we reached the top, we would visit the American Cemetery, a place that seemed both sad and romantic for me. Then we would run back downhill, pack up and make it home in time to watch Sunday Night at the London Palladium.

Sometimes we went to the coast but it was further and more expensive so only as a big treat. Boats ran from the banks of the Thames in London down the river and along the coast. Once we caught the boat to Canvey Island which I believed was the seaside only later to discover it was part of the Thames estuary. As I recall there was a small fairground and a sandy beach which we enjoyed. I begged for a pink sun hat with a ribbon with Canvey Island around it and eventually wore Mum and Dad down. All too soon it was time to catch the boat back, the wind had got up and it was a bit rough but Derek and I were running around the deck keeping warm when suddenly my hat blew off into the water. I sobbed and sobbed, it was so beautiful and now it was gone. Also on the deck was another family with lots of kids all in hats, the mother was massive and was sitting on the steps up to the other deck. She was so kind and took off her yellow hat and gave it to me, I remember being polite and thanking her but thinking that it couldn't compare with the pink one in any way.

As a family we loved speedway. Dad's younger brother, Uncle Bill, sometimes rode in races and Dad had also had a go but I don't think he was reckless enough to do well. We supported Wimbledon or the Dons as they were known. It was always a great evening to go there and meet up with Uncle Bill and his family who came up from Salisbury. We would eat proper hot dogs with onions and ketchup. I loved the smell of the oil burning, the best place to see and smell the race was on the first bend, that's where riders would throw themselves into the first corner to try and get ahead. We also went to a rough track called Rye House which was just made of red dust. If you sat on any of the bends you would be covered in dust flying up from the back wheels as they passed.

Dad loved it when family or friends came down from the north to London, the smoke. He would take time out to show them round the sights, not all of them were on the normal tourist route. I loved going out with them as I was developing a real love of history. Dad would drive past the Houses of Parliament, the Tower of London, pull up outside Buckingham Palace for a couple of minutes so we could look through the railings and check if the Queen was in by looking for the royal ensign flying above the building. We would go up to Oxford Street in the evening to watch the men who made glass animals in the big shops' doorways (I still have a love of glass.) We would buy hot chestnuts on cold nights to warm our hands and tummies. When My daughter was eleven, I asked my dad and mum to come down to London with us to show her around. We did all the usual things with Dad guiding from one major sight to another but also showing us things in between. He could tell us who every statue was that we passed, he pointed out the one up one down house that had been the smallest hospital in London and finally insisted on showing us cardboard city where many homeless go to sleep, as we drove down underground to it and saw the open fires where men and women were standing to keep warm I felt we had intruded too far. I insisted we leave and we were soon back up in our cosy world but I have never forgotten it.

Once, Keith and I decided to go to Thornton Reservoir, a local place with a lovely walk and, of course, the obligatory teashop. It took two of us to lift Mum's mobility scooter into the boot of the car. In fact, we had bought a different, bigger car to accommodate Mum and the scooter as we were both in danger of getting hernias trying to manipulate the scooter into the smaller car's limited boot space. So with the scooter packed, we set off for a brisk walk in the country. Mum noted the teashop immediately, so we promised we would walk around the reservoir and then call in. Mum set off at a brisk pace, the scooter had two settings: tortoise and hare, and it was definitely on hare! Keith and I were basically jogging to keep up! We asked Mum to slow down, but her sights were definitely on the refreshments. Then suddenly she did slow down because the battery was starting to lose power. Keith and I pushed Mum on the scooter for the last mile back to the café – we were all glad to get a cup of tea that day.

One of our happier outings was to watch Richard III's body arrive back in the city, ready to be reinterred. I'm keen on history and archaeology, so had followed the story of the discovery of the body in the car park. In fact, both Keith and

I have parked in that very car park when attending meetings in the city centre. We explained this to Mum and she became pretty interested in it all. When we heard that his body would pass quite nearby, we decided to go and watch. We left in plenty of time and found a great spot outside a pub. I managed to get us drinks just in time to see the hearse appear. People threw white roses in the road as the coffin passed. We enjoyed our trip out to salute history.

Another place Mum liked was a great local favourite, Bradgate Park. Mum could ride her scooter along the main pathway looking out for squirrels and deer. There were two cafes, one at either end of our route, but most of all, there were always children. She loved to see them on their bikes, in their buggies, scooting along or being carried on shoulders. She just loved children and could spend hours watching them. Once, a few years before, Keith and I had taken Mum and Dad to Southwold for a holiday. We found them a place to sit above the beach, near the pier, while we went for a walk. When we arrived back, Mum described everything that had happened on the beach. It included which family had built which sandcastles, who had swum, what the children had eaten and especially who she considered had been naughty and who had been good.

During this period while Mum lived at our house our second grandchild was born. Emma had been fit and healthy throughout her pregnancy and started labour on Thursday 19th August. She worked at the hospital and lived just a ten-minute walk away so knew there was no rush to get in but her labour didn't seem to develop. On the Friday she went for routine checks and was sent home in the hope that things would speed up. By Saturday she was having regular pains and Stan and Emma decided to go in to the labour ward. On arrival they found that there were no beds so they sat outside in the gardens waiting for things to progress. It was decided that labour wasn't progressing naturally so the staff would induce baby.

At this point Keith, who had his bag packed ready to drive down to Bristol decided he could wait no longer and set off. I wished I could go too but we couldn't leave Mum, she wasn't fit enough to travel, she's not been bothered to even get dressed for at least a week let alone sit in a car for over two hours. I stayed in Leicester planning to go down later when the first flush of visitors is over.

Baby Billy arrived on Sunday 23rd August but nothing was straight forward. Emma was induced and she was pushing for over an hour when they realised baby was on his side and wouldn't deliver, forceps were tried but eventually an emergency caesarean was offered. Billy was born but he wasn't breathing, it took two attempts to get him started, finally he did breathe and he was whipped off to the Baby Intensive Care Unit. When Stan eventually got a chance to phone Emma's mum, Beryl, he was distraught and basically unintelligible. Keith and Beryl plus Amy, who had also decided she needed to be in Bristol, rushed to the hospital but only Beryl was allowed in and then she also went silent. We were all thinking the worse but not saying it out loud. Keith was sending me texts which I read out to Mum and then forwarded to Ellie who was all the way down in Kent. What was going on? Why couldn't anyone text or phone us from the hospital? Had something unthinkable happened?

Then what seemed like hours and hours later Beryl phoned to say that Emma was fine although she had gone into shock and had been uncontrollably shaking and that Billy had had a seizure. The doctor in intensive care had placed him in a jacket designed to cool him down so that his brain activity would slow thus halting further fits. Billy had to wear it for 72 hours and then he would be gradually warmed up again.

Much later we received a short video of Billy in his magic jacket looking alert and gorgeous. Mum and I watched it over and over. We went to bed exhausted dreading receiving any calls during the night. I ached to be in Bristol but couldn't show that to Mum. She had been wonderful keeping my spirits up when we had bad news, telling me things would be all right and almost convincing me she was right.

Emma was in great pain after the birth but she was so resilient she did everything they asked of her. She wasn't allowed to see Billy until she walked to intensive care so she got out of bed and staggered to his unit! Keith rang after the trauma of the birth and we just cried together, neither of us said it but we were both thinking of what might have been, what would a world without Billy or Emma be like? On Tuesday Keith brought Amy home which meant that I could go down on Wednesday just for the day. I caught the train at 7.30 a.m., Ellie had driven over from Deal and was able to pick me up from the station, we went to Emma and Stan's first, it was full of baby things, so lovely!

We visited in the afternoon. First, we went to see Emma, she looked dreadful, totally washed out and obviously in great pain. I didn't tell her she looked fragile, I gave her a big hug and told her what a great job she was doing, it was hard not to cry but she was being strong so I felt I had to follow her lead. Then we all went through to see Billy. We had to leave bags, and coats outside and don gowns and wash our hands. Then we saw Billy. He was in his incubator all wired up to monitors and being chilled in his jacket. Emma was allowed to reach through a door on the side of the incubator and touch him, when she did, he opened his eyes and turned towards her. She told us that he had been distressed during the night, she had been fetched to touch him and he had calmed. He obviously knew her. It was so wonderful to see him at last; Ellie and I clung to each other and had a cry. We were allowed to stay for 15 precious minutes. Stan told us that they would start warming Billy up at 6 p.m. There was a risk that he could experience another fit, the warming would be completed over 12 hours. Ellie and I were allowed to be there with Stan and Emma when the process started. We watched Billy for a while until it was time for Stan and Emma to go to the day room to eat. Ellie and I both had to get home so we left hoping that everything would continue running smoothly. It did and by 3.30 a.m. we knew he was warm and alert! When I got back to Leicester,

Mum and I hugged. I wondered if she was thinking of her babies?

Keith and I were still checking out the building progress at Oak Court. We often drove past it on the way to the chemist, a place we now seemed to inhabit, as keeping up with Mum's medications was a full-time job. Dad had often told me it was a nightmare getting all their prescriptions sorted and now I could understand why. Mum took so many different tablets and some ran out at different times to others – suddenly she would tell us that she had no blood pressure tablets left or that her quinine was used up. We would have to dash to the doctors to get a prescription, then to the chemist to get it filled. Often the chemist would only have a handful of tablets and would write us an IOU for the rest which we would have to pick up on another day. I'm a great list writer and the chemist would be continually on my 'to-do list'. We also found that mistakes were made which made us realise that we needed to double check everything. We found our pharmacist, from a well-known chain who seemed to have cornered the market, inefficient and, at times, rude. The pharmacist would blame the doctor and then the doctor's receptionist would blame the pharmacy when all we wanted was the bloody tablets on time!

So we often made journeys to the doctors and/or the chemist and swung around to look at the building progress. Then, with horror, we realised work had ceased altogether. By doing a bit of research, Keith found out that there was an ongoing appeal against the building, being led by its neighbours. It seems that the main building had been built on the wrong part of the plot; it should have been at the back, whereas it was on the main road at the front. This meant that the three-storey building overlooked the neighbours' gardens. We couldn't believe it! We felt for the neighbours but were desperate for the building to continue. We held our breath for several weeks and then, with great relief, we noticed men on site again. We realised it would be delayed, but had no idea for how long.

Chapter 4
Diagnosis

As Oak Court started to get closer to being finished, we talked to Mum about making the decision to live there. First, she had to agree that she couldn't return to her own house, how would we get her to admit that was impossible. It was sorted when we decided to drive over to pick up some more clothes and belongings. We drove over and arrived on the drive on a cold autumn day. I felt anxious about how Mum would be, I was also aware of my own grief. I had been brought up here from the age of 14. We had had happy times here altogether – how would I cope seeing it empty of the life we'd lived?

I had lived in several houses as a child. After moving back from the Midlands, we ended up in Abourne Street in Paddington. We had two rooms and a landing. The landing was very important as this was our kitchen! The two rooms consisted of a living room, where everything except sleeping, happened. The second room was the bedroom for all four of us. Mum and Dad had a double bed and Derek and I slept in bunk beds, as the eldest Derek slept in the top bunk. To give Mum and Dad some privacy Dad erected a hardboard 'wall' to divide the room in half, because of fire regulations the 'wall' couldn't go up to the ceiling so it stopped a good two foot short. When we wanted to get up or to speak to our parents, we would pop our heads over. The living room wasn't big but it held a settee and two small chairs plus our dining table which was a cumbersome thing, very solid with big square legs. This left no room for cooking facilities so the cooker was set up on the landing outside the living room. To wash our pots, we had to carry them down in a bowl to the landing below where there was a deep sink with a draining board shared by several families.

Mum didn't seem to mind cooking on the landing though it wouldn't have suited me. I really don't like people in the kitchen when I'm cooking, Keith is an exception to this rule as he is so helpful. Mum however used to cook and chat to passing residents as they went up and down to their own flats. In this way she would know who was in. who was out, who was visiting and who wasn't, in other words she would know the gossip. I remember one pancake day we were all on the landing, Mum was mixing up the batter while Dad cooked and tossed the pancakes, Derek and I sat on the two top stairs ready to grab and eat the next one. I guess we were making a lot of noise so our neighbours were poking their heads out of their doors to join in. It seems to me that we stayed on that landing cooking pancakes until everyone in the house had eaten one plus my Uncle Bill Morgan who turned up on the off chance that food would be available. We ate them simply with just lemon and a sprinkle of sugar but they tasted divine.

When Dad was tossing the pancakes, he threw them up and over a small line that was also set up on the landing placed there for hanging 'smalls' on. Getting washing dry was always a problem as washing took place in the communal sink and then was hung out on a flat roof which was also one flight down. As no one had a washing machine or spin dryer clothes were generally dripping when they went on the line and so needed lots of sun or time to dry. Often clothes would be brought in damp and placed on clothes horses in the living room with underwear strung across the landing. Sometimes Mum and I would take a big wash to the launderette, we would pack it in the machine, put the wash powder in the top, turn the big dial and then wait. Sometimes Mum left me there while she went shopping or home to do something else. Then when the machine stopped, I would unload it into a plastic laundry basket and move it over to the tumble dryer. These were massive and I was quite scared of falling in one so I would load it carefully, put in the coins needed then shut the door which would start the motor. Many a time when I was emptying it into our bag to take home, I would find a jumper that had shrunk so much it would now struggle to fit a doll! Those machines were fierce. Once Mum decided I was old enough to go on my own, she gave me the washing and our powder which was cheaper than buying it there. I diligently put the washing in the machine and then I wasn't sure how much powder to put in never having done it alone before, I made a wild guess but overdid it. I watched in horror as the round window filled up with froth and then it started pouring out of the top where powder went in. Soon there was a bubble trail across the shop, luckily no one came in and eventually the froth started to subside. That was probably the cleanest washing we had ever had.

Our flat and the others in the house were not designed for a growing family, in the summer and on any dry days we played out. The house had a massive front door step and we often played just on that. I loved to play hairdressers and I would set the step up as Pam's Salon complete with bowls of water, a seat for sitting on and accessories like my mum's spiky rollers and perm paraphernalia. I also liked playing school and would often have several friends sitting on the step complete with bits of paper and pencils. My brother was more likely to be found riding his bike or roller skating down the hill or at the Red Rec, our local recreation ground. I have no idea why it was called Red; I can't remember any colour there just a lot of rough grass. When it was fine, we also played on the flat roof underneath the washing, this was not popular with those who had washing hanging out but I had a little tub plus washing board which I used while Mum did our real washing, I would get all our handkerchiefs and socks to wash, I did it very diligently.

When it was wet or too cold, we would have to stay in-doors but we would have to be quiet. At the time my dad was trying to qualify to be a London cabbie, a taxi driver. To do this he had to learn 'the knowledge'. This meant that he had to memorise every road, street, alleyway, landmark, hotel etc. in London. On the wall above our dining table was a map of London showing the course of the river Thames and all the streets, it was mind boggling. Dad had grown up in London but there were areas he knew very little about so several days a week he would go out on his moped, which everyone called a noddy bike, to check out a different section of the map. Sometimes he would do this in a group with other trainees and sometimes he would go alone. He would set off in the early morning and arrive home tired out often as we were going to bed. When he wasn't on the streets, he would be at home sitting at the table with a notebook, studying the map. He also had a book of questions that the examiners would ask him at his next assessment. I used to love reading the questions out to him and trying to follow his answer to see if he got it right. I was a good reader and listener. Every so often he would go up to the testing station and face one of the examiners. They would ask him three questions from the book, something like: "How do you get from Kings Cross Station to Tower Bridge." Dad told us that they were strict and enjoyed seeing men fail. One of them actually told Dad that he would never pass, this made Dad even more determined, he wasn't a great reader and had had little formal schooling but he had a great sense of direction and a good memory for roads so eventually he did pass, the map came down and Dad started work for a governor driving taxis at nights, that gave him loads more stories to tell us as he often drove celebrities and other London characters.

So on days when we were all squeezed in to the house Derek and I had to be very quiet. I loved reading, drawing and colouring. Derek was harder to please as he wasn't as academic as me but he did like drawing in a more technical way. He would draw cars or just 3D shapes. He loved sport from an early age and collected cigarette cards of his favourite players. There was almost four years between us so we didn't always get on, I felt he was 'bossing me' because I was younger, he felt he was telling me things for my own good. After two or three wet days in a row we would probably be almost insufferable so Dad would take us and our friends from the street for a ride in the cab. I remember times when there were too many of us to fit on the seats so us little ones would sit on the bigger kids' laps. If anyone saw a policeman they shouted 'bluebottle' and we would all fall to the floor. Often, we would end up at Hampstead Heath where Dad would let us all out and we would run off our energy while he sat on a bench on top of the heath having a cigarette or two. Then we would all pile back in and come home.

Once Dad started driving a cab and earning what he described as 'good money' we became upwardly mobile. First, we moved to a flat on Warwick Avenue, here Derek and I had a bedroom each and we had our first bathroom! Before this we had bathed in a tin bath which hung on the wall on the flat roof for the rest of the week. On Fridays Dad would get the bath down and put it in the living room then Mum would fill it up from the immersion and by boiling kettles. I was lucky as the smallest I would get to take a bath first, then the water would be topped up for Derek. Once we two were in bed Mum would top the bath up again and get herself clean. Dad got the privileged of walking to the Porchester Baths with a small rolled up towel containing a sliver of soap where he would join the queue of men waiting to use the hip baths. If I got dirty during the week I would be taken to the communal sink where I would sit on the draining board and be given a wash down. So moving to somewhere with a bath was a real step up for us.

On the way to Immingham I found myself remembering all these homes we had lived in, remembering all the love we had shared as a family. Now we were getting close how would I feel about being back at this one? When we unlocked the back door, the cold slammed us in the face. The boiler had broken down! My brother had been there the day before to put the heating on and it was working when he left, but no longer! We got Mum into the front room and put the kettle on, along with the fire and any other heaters we could find. Keith tried to get the boiler going but to no avail, the helpful phone numbers stuck on the side of the boiler, all in Dad's handwriting, were all out of date. It was a Sunday; there was nothing we could do. There was no time to get emotional, we all had to use all our energy to keep warm while grabbing the things we needed! Once Mum had told us what she needed, she went off next door to talk to her neighbour and have another hot drink. Keith and I were miserable and very cold! Finally, we got everything in the car, there was a bit of space so Keith rescued a couple of Mum's large pot plants from the back garden that were on the verge of giving up the ghost. We got Mum back in the car and drove home. No time to be sentimental! As we were nearing Leicester, Mum suddenly said, "I can't live there anymore." We agreed, then drove the last few miles in thoughtful silence – I was so relieved.

We did wonder if Mum would say she wanted to continue living with us, but she didn't. She was unhappy being reliant on us; she never treated her space as hers. She didn't keep it tidy or clean it or put out any of her things. I did all of that. She needed her own place and we believed Oak Court was it. However, we had to get Mum assessed by Social Care before we could apply for a place. We were all there when a youngish woman visited to talk to Mum. Of course, she had a long form to fill out, but she made it as pleasant as she could, engaging Mum in conversation first, listening to what Mum had to say about her own house. Mum agreed that her house would have to be sold. Now that she had decided she couldn't go back, she seemed very accepting about it going. She hoped a family would buy it, someone with children. In fact, the couple that bought it were pregnant and had twins – Mum was very pleased about this when we told her.

The Social Care woman had to check whether Mum qualified for sheltered accommodation. She not only needed to check Mum's ability to live alone but also her need for some support. We were nervous that we had got it wrong and we became even more worried when Mum decided to tell her that she could do everything for herself! She insisted that she could clean, do her own washing, make her bed and prepare food! We were struck dumb and could see her chances of getting a flat disappearing down the plughole, but this woman was cannier than that. Initially, she seemed to accept Mum's answers but then she would return to each one asking more questions. Could Mum clean behind the furniture? Could she reach up to clean the dust off pictures? Could she hang washing on a line? She also watched Mum very carefully when she went to the toilet. She saw how she 'furniture-walked', resting her hands and arms on each piece of furniture on the short journey from the sitting room to the toilet. Finally, she declared that Mum was a perfect candidate for Oak Court! That evening when Keith and I went out for our quick walk together, we were almost jumping with joy!

the deck to find they were in the middle of a minefield he roof was going on at Oak Court but the inside was just one big space. How long would it take to make 50 kitchens and bathrooms along with all the communal spaces, we asked ourselves.

Then fate took over again. In early spring, Mum woke us up in the night. We had bought a panic button as her bedroom was downstairs and we slept upstairs. She had never used it until now. It was loud; I awoke in total panic and almost hurled myself down our very steep and narrow stairs. Mum had pressed the button because she had terrible pains in her back. We tried painkillers and a hot drink but she couldn't settle, so we called the doctor. While we were waiting for the doctor to arrive, I rehearsed Mum so that she would be able to say what was wrong. She wasn't very good at communicating exactly what was going on with her body – she would be diverted by something small and forget the big stuff. It didn't surprise me when she suddenly said, "Do you think I should show the doctor my breast?" I was about to tell her not to when I thought to ask what it was about her breast that the doctor might be interested in. She then showed me her breast. I tried not to gasp as her breast had an inverted nipple, it also had a lot of puckering in the tissue.

I felt sick as I recognised two of the signs of breast cancer. How long had she had it, I wondered. We decided we would show the doctor her breast. The doctor was a lovely, young woman, the same one that had asked Mum about being resuscitated when we thought she was bleeding internally. At first, she checked Mum's back and then as she was about to leave, I reminded Mum about her breast. When Mum opened her nightie, the doctor looked at me – she knew I knew that this was likely to be serious. Mum was oblivious but agreed that she would go to the hospital to have it checked. So began a long and frightening journey.

A week later, we were at the Breast Care Centre, waiting in a busy waiting area with many other anxious women. Mum, at 90, was the oldest there. She was starting to realise that this could be serious. The staff were wonderful. We helped Mum stand for the mammogram and then a very kind nurse explained that they were also going to carry out an ultra sound scan. I accompanied Mum into both. She was so brave and patient. Lying flat on her back hurt her, but she bore it. Then they said they wanted to do a couple of biopsies. That hurt Mum; she squeezed my hand but didn't murmur. I was amazed as she usually complained about hospitals and made a fuss.

The week's wait for the results seemed endless. Mum didn't talk about it and I didn't want to bring it up if she didn't want to, so we sat in silence, no doubt, each with our own fears. When we returned to the clinic, they confirmed that it was breast cancer; Mum had probably had it for at least a year, if not two. Mum cried quiet tears. I had to stay strong, I felt I couldn't lose control. I had to be strong for her as she had been strong for me when I was a child. Medication was prescribed to keep the cancer in check and a mastectomy was offered. Mum was to have time to think it over. We left feeling stunned, pole-axed.

In the weeks that followed, the questions Mum most wanted answering were "Why me?" and "What did I do to get this?" It was hard to explain that nothing she had done had caused it – how do you explain something that isn't truly understood yet? Sometimes, she would say that she would have the mastectomy and at other times, she would cry and say that she didn't want surgery. She asked everyone what she should do. I felt very strongly that she should decide for herself – looking back I realise that Mum needed Dad to help her and as I was his replacement, she needed me to decide for her, something I wouldn't do out of principle. It was cruel for Mum and she agonised over the decision. Eventually, she decided she would have the operation. We were all prepared when she got an infection, fell ill and when she recovered, felt so weak that she changed her mind. Finally, she decided to trust in the medication and get on with life.

When she felt stronger, my brother took her to see Oak Court again, and by chance, they talked with the manager. Mum was able to choose her own flat; she chose a flat on the ground floor that had patio doors where she hoped to sit outside. It was on the front of the building, so she could watch people going past. Even though she had made this choice, I overheard her telling my aunt Dot on the phone that she wasn't looking forward to moving in. For a while, she refused to talk to us at all, let alone about moving – these were difficult times.

Chapter 5
The Good Life

Finally, the day came when we were told Mum could move in, she would get her flat, after over 12 months since my dad had died and she had first come to live with us. Suddenly, it was all 'hurry up'!

We had to take a last trip to Lincolnshire to decide what would come to the new flat and what would have to go. This was going to be a big job that could be distressing for us all as we all had memories of Immingham stretching back years. Many of the objects in the house held precious memories, but Mum was moving from a three-bedroom house with a shed and a garage to a one-bed flat with limited storage! We already had boxes in our garage belonging to my daughter, that had moved about 12 times during her college days and early jobs to different destinations. We had downsized our house and had limited space ourselves, so we were going to have to be pretty brutal. Could Mum rise to the challenge?

We developed a system that involved Mum sitting on a chair in each room while Keith and I collected and held up items almost like an auction. Mum would say 'yes', 'no' or 'maybe'. 'Yes' meant it was definitely coming, 'no' meant it was going in the charity bags and 'maybe' meant it was going in a reserve box in our garage in case it was missed later. We worked our way through the house and shed, unearthing caches of inner soles, sets of pegs and enough plasters to supply an accident-prone football team or two!

Mum behaved as if she had wiped her memory clean – she didn't seem at all sentimental about most of the objects, photos and furniture. I kept checking that she was OK and she assured us that she was. I put things in the 'keep' box that she was prepared to give away.

The mound for the charity shop grew and grew, we had agreed that we would just walk away at the end of the day and that my brother would take everything locally after we'd gone. My brother also volunteered to clear the garage. I didn't envy him the task; my dad had saved every scrap of wood, every piece of metal, every screw or nail that he could in that garage. He always believed that one day each one of them would prove useful, now those days had run out.

We used to laugh and Mum would pull a face when he came back from the trip, bearing more than he had taken with him! However, some things did prove useful. When Ellie was a little girl, Mum and Dad got her a tiny pram made with a metal frame and brown corduroy body. She loved it! Nestling underneath was a lovely rack to hold her shopping or baby bag, fashioned out of a supermarket basket that Dad had picked up somewhere! As my dad got older and wasn't allowed to drive a car, he progressed to having a mobility scooter. Eventually, he made a trailer for that scooter to carry the shopping and to carry things to, and more importantly, back from the tip.

When we left Immingham for the last time, Mum sat comfortably in the back of our car. As Keith drove us back, I thought of how I had left this house years before to start college in Sheffield, to train as a teacher, a dream come true. My parents supported me through school even though neither of them had good educational experiences. Dad used to tell stories of children coming to school with no shoes on their feet who were picked on by the sometimes brutal teachers. Dad himself was caned and often given the slipper and told he was stupid. Mum had liked school but coming from quite a large family she didn't get the opportunity to stay on, instead she had the take a job to put money in the family purse.

When we moved to Immingham, I had to change schools, I travelled 12 miles each morning and another twelve to come home again each evening so that I could go to the grammar school in Cleethorpes. Moving schools just as I had started my GCSE year could have been disastrous but in fact I did well out of it. The staff of any subject where I had been following a different curriculum provided me with extra one to one tuition to bring me up to speed. The school was a happy place and I made good friends, I did well and was expected to go to University. When my A' level results came through, I was working at the Findus frozen food factory on nights, Mum woke me up when she saw the self-addressed envelope arrive. I took one look at the grades and realised I had missed out by one grade in one subject. I turned over and went back to sleep, Mum fretted until Dad came home and then they woke me up to talk. I didn't know what to say so I went for a long walk round then caught a bus to Grimsby called in at the Education Department and took a temporary one-year job as an ancillary in an infant school. I had bought myself a year. I believed that I wanted to be a teacher and I thought this was a good way of being sure. The pay was poor, it would cover my bus fares for the eighteen-mile round trip each day plus about half as much again as pocket money.

I spent the year working with some very experienced teachers, I learnt so much from them about working with young children. I admired them and I wanted to be like them. By Christmas I had got myself a place at Teacher Training College, my parents couldn't have been any more proud. The following September they drove me over to my hall of residence in Sheffield.

By the time I qualified with a degree, four years later, I was married and my husband and I were looking for two jobs in the same authority. Leicester became our home. Dad and Derek hired a van in Immingham, collected odd bits of furniture from neighbours and friends then drove to Sheffield to pick up the rest of our stuff. Then we all drove on to Leicester. Never one to spend money when it could be saved my brother had hired the van for one day so it had to be back in Lincolnshire by 5 p.m. All was going well until the last item a large, old-fashioned, double wardrobe that had been donated to us. It was the only bedroom storage we had. As we tried to take it into the small terrace house, we realised that it would not go up the stairs. Dad suggested taking it up the outside of the house and in through the bedroom window which was a large bay. Even so the wardrobe was too big, we would have to do it in two parts. When we looked, the two halves were held together by numerous screws all of which were rusted and were never going to move. It looked like we would have to abandon the venture. Then Dad took out his saw and began to saw down the back of the wardrobe through all the batons holding it together. Time was tight, we had to get it in within the next five minutes. My husband and I ran upstairs and leaned as far out of the window as possible, Derek and Dad heaved the first half of the wardrobe up and we grabbed and held it while they raced inside, up the stairs and then grabbed the item and helped us pull it in. This was repeated with the other piece, then they jumped into the van and motored off home, just in time to claim their full deposit back. We were in! We both started work in Leicestershire, my husband in the county and me in the city.

This time it was me moving Mum, everything that would be following on was at one end of the living room waiting for Derek to bring it over. All of Mum's worldly goods came down the M1 in just a single van.

The following week, Keith and I went to the flat every day to sort out the furniture, put things in cupboards, make the bed, put up curtains and finally, to hang the photos and place the ornaments. I wasn't sleeping, I would get up at night and prowl around our house, worrying. What would we do if she refused to go? What if she moved in but didn't like it? We couldn't have her back, but how could we insist she live there?

In the early hours of the morning, it was clear I needed a plan; a plan to introduce her to Oak Court. This plan was delayed several times as Mum had a series of minor illnesses; a heavy cold, a bout of diarrhoea, a pain in her stomach. I believed that it was all due to her anxiety, but how could we challenge that? We just had to sit tight and wait.

In the interim, Mum had an appointment at the hospital to check her breast cancer. Fingers crossed, this will be good news and won't affect her going to live independently. It is good news; the medication has shrunk the cancer! We go to the tearooms to celebrate. The next day Mum is ill again with awful diarrhoea. It takes us a few days to find out that she has C difficile a virulent infection possibly picked up in the hospital or from one of the numerous health practitioners who didn't wear gloves when visiting our home. We have to wash everything and wipe all surfaces down continually so that we don't get it. We are exhausted and can't let anyone visit us, including our granddaughter, in case they get it. We think it has gone and then Mum gets another dose – she is worn out and cries. The whole of September and October have passed and Mum is still with us. During this time, Mum's house sale has fallen through – we are demoralised.

Finally, in early November, we see an opportunity, Mum is well, the flat is ready and I advance my plan. For several days before Mum's new moving date, I take Mum to Oak Court to check out the flat or drop something off. We always have a look around and a couple of times, have been lucky enough to bump into residents who I engage in conversation! On a couple of occasions, we have stayed for lunch and I have muscled in on a half full table, introducing myself and Mum. The other women are lovely and welcoming, they have only recently moved in themselves so must know how Mum feels. Their ages vary from about 58 to late 80s, Mum will be the second oldest woman there at 91, she is proud of this especially as any staff she tells quickly say that she doesn't look her age! They are right, she doesn't.

On the day before Mum moves in, Keith and I take her over for lunch. We are all going to stay and as we arrive, I look for a table, but Mum is being called over by a woman we have met before on one of our visits. Mum hesitates and a member of the kitchen staff rushes over to settle her and to place us on a table for two around a corner; it's wonderful, we can clearly hear Mum telling the other women about her house in Lincolnshire and then we hear her say something, we're not sure what, and everyone laughs. I want to cry, suddenly I know this is going to work.

The next day, Mum moves in; I go and fetch her some shopping before she gets up so that she can have fresh fruit, milk and some little treats. We go over to Oak Court in time for lunch. I don't stay but drop her off and see her into the dining room where she heads straight for 'her table'. I go back later to find her back in her flat watching TV, she tells me what she's going to have for tea. We embrace and I walk away down the corridor with the brand-new carpet and I can't believe this has happened. That night Keith and I go for an Indian meal in the village. We spend the whole evening talking about Mum and hoping she will be OK on this first night away. Neither of us sleep that well.

Very soon, a pattern evolved. I visited Mum almost every day, it became a pleasure as she had things to tell me. I would stay for lunch at least once a week, sometimes both Keith and I would stop for Sunday lunch. On Thursdays, I would collect Mum and we would go for a pub lunch. Mum always had a main and a pudding, she was working her way down the desserts menu. Mondays I shopped for Mum and took it over to put in her cupboards, on most days she ate tea in her own room so I always bought her some treats like dressed crab, gala pie and bacon! On Wednesdays, there was bingo in the afternoon, Mum loved bingo and they also had a raffle where everyone won something small. Perfect! So on Wednesdays, I had a day off knowing she had something to do that would bring her into contact with others. Weekends were quiet, so sometimes if the weather was good and she was up to it, we would take Mum out usually for coffee and cake.

On Tuesdays, we looked after our granddaughter, Lilli. After lunch, we would put her in her buggy and take her down to see the ducks at our park and from there, up to Oak Court to see 'Nanny Win'. I had supplied Mum with a crate of toys which came out from the cupboard under the sink.

Mum supplied herself with biscuits from the small shop on the site. We would all have a drink and Mum would insist on feeding Lilli Jammy Dodgers or custard creams. Of course, Lilli loved it. Sometimes, we would go in the shared lounge or out in the gardens where the other residents were always very happy to talk to Lilli. Mum was proud and loved it. When our grandson, Billy, came up from Bristol, he was a favourite with everyone too. Once Mum had him on her three-wheel rollator taking him up the corridor and he was laughing – I think of that afternoon often and how much fun it was.

Our three girls visited Mum and were always welcomed and Mum had other visitors. Once, my nephew and his wife brought their two children up from Hertfordshire. We had planned a picnic in the park, but Mum was unwell, a bit of tummy trouble. Instead we had the picnic on the floor of Mum's flat! The children Emily and Thomas kept Mum amused throughout the visit and were a topic of conversation for days after they'd gone home.

There were also special times at Oak Court. With Christmas coming, there was a fete. I decided that Mum and I would throw ourselves in to this event and run a stall. As Mum loved children, I decided we would sell pocket money toys. I stocked up and on the day, we had a variety of small toys and trinkets. I persuaded Mum to wear her Christmas jumper and we both wore dangly, shiny earrings and Rudolf antlers! Our stall was directly opposite Santa, so we were able to watch as the children went in for their visit. We saw Lilli being so shy we couldn't believe it and we also saw Santa grab the manager of the place and pull her on his knee for a big kiss! Mum loved it and loved telling everyone afterwards that it was OK as he was her fiancé! Our family Christmas was redesigned to suit Mum and her new circumstances. I picked her up and we all met at Andy and Amy's house for a grand family lunch with about 14 of us there. Mum loved the meal, cooked by us all at our own homes and then brought together for everyone to share. She saw the children playing with their toys and when she was tired, I took her back to her flat where we had a cup of tea together before I left. This was almost repeated on Boxing Day, except that the venue was our place.

I tried to replicate the family love and fun we had experienced as children. Mum and Dad had always bought my brother and me presents which we found in pillowcases at the end of our beds. We also hung up one of Dad's socks every year which was filled with small treats like sweets and marbles, with the obligatory bag of gold coins and a satsuma shoved down into the toe. Whatever our family circumstances, and there must have been times when there was very little money to spare, we were satisfied.

I was born on 18 November 1952 at home in in Oxford Square. It sounds posh but it was in fact one of a large number of flats forming part of a Victorian House abandoned during the war. The occupants moved out and never returned. Our flat was dark and poky but Dad once told me that one day when he passed another house on the square the door was open. Being Dad, he poked his nose inside and came across a 'gentleman' who was just leaving. Again being Dad, he introduced himself and wangled an invite to take a look inside. What he found was a glimpse of another lost world. On the first floor there was just a single room which was lined by beautiful mirrors and the room contained just a single piece of furniture – a black, grand piano. The property was being stripped of its former glory to provide flats for the growing number of families like ours.

Soon after I was born, I became ill with gastroenteritis and was admitted to St Mary's Hospital where I was placed in an incubator in a window. I was to remain there until they were sure I would thrive. My Dad was driving lorries at the time and every journey he made now went via St Mary's so that he could look up at the window to check I was still there. On one occasion the cot was empty, parking the lorry on the pavement he ran inside and up the stairs fearing the worst only to find that I was dressed and ready to go home. Even so the specialist spoke to Dad and told him that as a fragile baby I needed fresh air and recommended a move to the countryside. Dad's Aunt Mag lived in a small village in Warwickshire so after some negotiations we took up residence there. We lived in what looked like an idyllic, chocolate-box cottage complete with thatched roof.

This meant I spent the first three years of my life in the country. My memories are vague but I remember a beautiful, wild meadow and lots of sun. I have photos of myself as a blonde, curly-haired toddler picking flowers and of my big brother, Derek, riding a massive pig. There was a lake and we played and swam in it. Mum grew vegetables, she always had 'green fingers' and she also kept chickens which I was frightened of, I think I once wandered in to their pen on my own and got chased out! Even now I'm scared of most birds and can't stand feathers either! I did have my own pet though. Mum was busy keeping house and my brother had started at the village school so I was sometimes left to my own devices with the run of the house. One day Mum came in from hanging out the washing and found me with the pantry open trying to pour some milk in a saucer, she was intrigued so she stayed quiet to watch what I would do next. I carefully carried the saucer of milk upstairs where I stood on a chair to push the saucer up into the rafters. When Mum asked what I was up to, it became clear that I thought there was a kitten that lived in the thatching, Mum quickly concluded that this wasn't an imaginary pet but more likely a rat! Soon after this Mum convinced Dad that I was no longer a fragile child and we upped sticks and moved on to a more urban environment! Our sojourn in the country was over.

Life at Oak Court was good; Mum liked her flat, she liked the food, she had made friends and she trusted the staff who liked her and understood her sense of humour. She's had an early fall which ended up as an all-night visit to A&E but she's recovered well and back on her feet. In fact she has now been assessed for aids which make life easier for her and us. Keith and I are starting to get our lives back into order. Then fate played its next card. Once more the rug was pulled out from under us and I fell flat on my smiling face. On the photo from Christmas we're all smiling but Keith and

I are keeping a big secret, one that will affect the whole family, one that scares us so much we try not to talk about it, one that makes us hold each other close in the dark of our bedroom.

Chapter 6
Downward Slide

Tuesday, 15 December 2015

Mum seems to be recovering from her fall, although her ankle is still infected where she grazed it and lay on the bathroom floor. She can't go out, so I'm visiting as often as I can but I'm also managing to get some Christmas shopping done. Tonight, Keith and I are going to get children's presents, including Lilli and Billy's; we're looking forward to choosing for them! Ellie and I have agreed to meet on Saturday the 19th at Windsor. It should be very Christmassy and it's half way between Leicester and Deal; so a good venue. Last time we were here was when Ellie was about seven and I took her to see the Queen's Doll's House; we both want to do that again!

Thursday, 17 December

I'm sitting in the front room, it is about 2 a.m. About an hour ago, I woke up and found a large lump in my left breast. I'm waiting for surgery to open so that I can phone for an appointment. I'm not sure what woke me up, but I felt uncomfortable. I thought Lilli might have dropped one of Keith's shells or stones in the bed, she loves playing with them. Then I realised that this lump was inside me. I'm scared, this is our next piece of bad luck. I'm pretty certain this is cancer it is so big. I don't want this to spoil 2016 – we were looking forward to doing lots of things now Mum is settled. I'm also scared that I will die. How can I sleep?

Later – I've been to the doctor and saw my own GP and a student. The student looked petrified when he examined me and I knew what he was thinking. I've been referred to the breast clinic, I will get an appointment within two weeks. I've looked at my breast and I can now see a dimple in the skin that worries me. Keith says it is a cyst. I can't tell whether he is saying that to make me feel better or whether he really believes it. I have decided not to tell anyone else until I know more. The waiting is going to be hard.

Friday, 18 December

Surprisingly I managed to get some sleep last night. Today I have been in two worlds; in one I'm preparing for Christmas by finishing my wrapping and writing my food shopping lists. I've also visited Mum and stayed for lunch. In my other darker world, I'm preparing for the worse. I'm thinking about dying and what I have to do before that happens; what can I do to make sure Elle will be OK, what about Mum, how will Keith manage?

Monday, 21 December

My double life continues. On Saturday, I met Elle in Windsor. The weather was great; crisp and cold and sunny. We enjoyed going around the castle and remembered things that happened when we visited last, just after the big fire. At that time, Prince Charles was visiting and he waved at Elle who was just a little girl. There were parts of the castle that were closed due to smoke damage, but this time we got to see it all, including another look at the doll's house. We also looked in loads of shops, though we didn't buy anything much except an outfit for Lilli!!! Several times, we talked about the future and I found it difficult not to tell her about my breast, I'm absolutely useless at lying but I can 'fib' for a good cause, so I did.

When I'm not with people, I slide into the other dimension. I can now feel the lump all the time, as if it is tormenting me. I just want to know what it is and what is going to happen. Not knowing is difficult. I'm a person who likes to be in control and I can't be. My appointment has come through for 30th December.

Sunday, 27 December

Christmas is over. We got together as a family this year at Amy and Andy's house, there were 13 of us and we all cooked something towards the meal. I cooked the vegetables and trimmings. The house was bedlam when we arrived, full of toys and with three excited children, two of them our grandchildren! Generally, it went well. Mum and I wore Christmas jumpers and everyone had hats. A group photo was taken and we're all smiling out at the camera. I look at it and realise what a great job Keith and I were doing, what a cover up! Just under the surface I was thinking this could be my last Christmas and that I needed to fix it in my brain somehow to hang on to when the worse times come. I knew that Keith was doing something similar.

Thursday, 31 December

New Year's Eve, and we're getting ready to go out to a big dinner dance with our friends Dave and Marie. I went to the clinic yesterday and it pretty much went exactly as I'd feared it would. I knew the ropes, having been with both Mum and a dear friend, and having two friends who've had breast cancer. First, the Macmillan nurse examined me and as soon as she said that I would be having a mammogram plus ultra sound and a biopsy, I knew she thought it was cancer. Usually, they just do one thing at a time. Keith was still sticking to his cyst diagnosis, so I had to tell him that things didn't look good. Everyone was very kind and gentle. Finally, we went back to the Macmillan nurse who told us it would take a week for the results. I pushed her and she, more or less, told us that they all thought it was cancer, and that they would want to act quickly. I looked at Keith and my heart went out to him, it was obvious he had thought it was a cyst, a false alarm.

We have decided to tell Dave and Marie that we think I have cancer. I don't think either of us can go tonight and keep up the show at midnight when everyone is shouting: "Happy New Year." We are going to go, but at midnight we will need a few minutes on our own.

Friday, 1 January 2016

I have never written a New Year entry with so much going on inside my head. So much of it is pure, raw fear. We have entered a new year and we don't know what we will have to face and whether we will come through it. Will this be my last Christmas, my last New Year? It is our tradition to pack our Christmas decorations away early in the New Year – we never wait for Twelfth Night, so I got on with it. As I packed away the tree baubles, I was crying – here were Eleanor's baby baubles and things she'd made at school, who would get them out next year? Who would keep Elle's baby memories alive if I wasn't here to do it?

Thursday, 7 January

We have been to Bristol to visit Emma, Stan and Billy. It was good to go, partly because I wasn't sure when I would get there again and partly because being part of a busy household made time pass quickly. I decided to drive back as I thought it would occupy my mind. Big mistake as we pulled into the services, I managed to clip someone's car! I burst into tears! Luckily, they weren't bothered, I guess it was a company car.

Our appointment at the clinic was at teatime. We met the consultant who told us that it was cancer and that it was in the lymph node they had biopsied. The tumour is big and fast growing. She made it clear that her advice was to have a mastectomy as soon as possible. None of this surprised me, though there was a part of me that was holding out a glimmer of hope, that it wouldn't be this way. The consultant, who was so calm and confident that she made me calm and confident, had a brief private conversation with my Macmillan nurse. Then they returned with an offer; if I felt up to it, the consultant would do the operation on the following Monday, I accepted. We arrived home at 7.30 p.m., knowing that we now had the hard job of telling the girls.

We did it all by phone, as both Ellie and Em were too far away for us to 'pop over'. How do you tell someone you love something positive when you are feeling so frightened yourself? As a parent, I had always tried to shield Ellie and then Amy and Emma and now, we had to tell them something that would frighten them. It wasn't easy, but we did it and they phoned each other for comfort.

I also had to tell my mum. At first, she cried, but then she had a very strange reaction; it was as if she felt I was in competition with her! She was also angry that I hadn't told her first, it was as if she believed there was a protocol which said 'Mothers first'!

E-mail sent from my iPad

8 January 2016 3.10 am
Just wanted to let you all know that I am going into hospital this Monday (11th) to have a mastectomy. I found a lump in my breast just before Xmas. I was referred to Glenfield and went last week where I had various assessments. Yesterday I went back and it was confirmed as cancer. I was offered the op quickly and I accepted. Hopefully, I will be out on Tuesday. Then I will probably have various other treatments – chemo, radiotherapy, etc. Not what I wanted in 2016, but there is no other choice really. It has been hard telling the girls plus my mum who was diagnosed at about this time last year! Keith has been wonderful as ever.

I will update you next week when I am back home.

Pam x

P.S. If you think I have missed anybody off this list, please forward my e-mail to them. Thanks.

Sent from my iPad.

I'm waiting to go to bed. I have to be at the hospital at 7 a.m. tomorrow for my operation. Keith isn't here. Life has been hell since my diagnosis. The day after, I had to go and have all my pre op stuff, like blood tests. Keith then took me shopping for nightwear and a soft bra with a mastectomy pocket to hold some sort of prosthetic. I had to have something that I can get on and off easy for on the ward; I should only be in one night but they will need to examine me! I also bought non-scented toiletries as I won't be able to use my normal stuff in the wound area. We decided to go for a coffee and Keith bumped into some people we know. I can't believe I did this, but I hid behind a display so that they wouldn't see me – luckily the display was a large cardboard cut-out of Chewbacca from Star Wars, so I was well hidden! I just couldn't talk to anyone; we had to leave our coffees and exit stage left very quickly!

I've had to make decisions about who to tell. I've decided that as I can't control what is happening to me, I do want to control what and how people are told. Years ago when Keith had a heart bypass, I found myself answering the phone anytime from 7 a.m. until 11 p.m. I didn't want that for Keith, so I decided that e-mail would be my chosen method of communication for everyone, except very close family. I sent out the first of a series of e-mails to friends and colleagues. Luckily, I'm already retired, so I didn't have to sort out work issues. I've taken leave from my charity work.

This afternoon, we went to see my mum. Keith came too and I was so glad because she was vile to me. We went for lunch and sat with her and her friends and that was OK, but as soon as we went to her room, she began to ignore me – the atmosphere turned 'Arctic'! I tried to make small talk but to no avail, so we decided to leave. She didn't even wish me luck. I can only think that she is so frightened about me and about what will happen to her that she can't deal with it at all and this is her reaction.

We came home, but a couple of hours later we got a call to say she was complaining of pains and had told the carers that she had fallen yesterday. They were calling for an ambulance. Keith had to go over and accompany her to hospital, leaving me here. Not what either of us wanted.

Tuesday, 12 January

I'm back home! Keith didn't get back until 2 a.m. on Monday morning; Mum had been admitted to the Infirmary. We made it to the Breast Care Unit for 7 a.m. and I went down for my mastectomy at about 9.30. I surprised myself by being calm, I've never been in hospital except when Ellie was born, so it was all new to me. My surgeon came to see me, she was smiling and confident. I hate things over my face, so I remember the little panic when the oxygen mask went on, then I was back in the recovery room.

Keith came to see me at about 2.30, he had come from seeing Mum who was being troublesome and demanding to go home. No sooner had he arrived than he had a call from Mum's ward saying she was trying to get dressed and would he speak to her! This was insane – we could hear Mum shouting in the background, saying that Keith should leave me to go to her. Keith phoned my brother who took over communication with Mum's carers and arrived the next day to get her home. Afterwards, when all of this was over, Mum never spoke about what had gone on; it was as if she had wiped it from her memory.

12 January 2016 16.06
This is a general update – some of you may know some of this already, but some may not.

I had op early on Monday morning – We had to be at the hospital at 7 a.m. We had planned a quiet Sunday but that wasn't to be, as in the late afternoon my mum started complaining of pains. The sheltered accommodation were concerned as she had fallen a couple of days before, but seemed OK at the time. So after calling out medics, it was decided that she needed to go to the hospital for X-rays. Poor Keith ended up at A&E until 2.30 a.m. when she was finally admitted, mainly because she had got high blood pressure by then! He then returned home ready to take me!

The op went well. I have had no real pain to speak of. I had one night in the hospital. Luckily, I had a side room, so it was pretty quiet. I had my own loo too which was good 'cos I had to drink a lot. This morning they got me ready to discharge, which meant loads of checks etc. I also have a cushion to shove in my bra! Very fetching! I am now at home. I have a drain still attached which is cramping my style a bit, but generally I feel much better than I thought I would.

Coincidentally, Mum has also been discharged today. She was very troublesome in hospital and they say there is nothing wrong with her! My brother was coming to visit to-day, so we have left him to get her home and settled down! The plan is for him to bring her to see me tomorrow, if she and I are up to it.

So the op is over. I have 3 weeks to heal, then I go back to hear what the next part of my plan is. It will probably in-clude chemo and radiotherapy, so I know I need to rest and get strong.

Keith has been wonderful; caring without smothering. The girls are all coming to see me over the next few days... I just wanted Keith yesterday and today. Thanks for all your messages which have cheered me to no end. I won't be call-ing anyone yet, as I'm still too tired and there are so many of you... so calls are for close family at the moment. I know you will all understand. I expect to have ups and downs but will keep in touch.

Pam x

PS If you want to pass this on to anyone else, please feel free!

Sent from my iPad.

Chapter 7
Recovery

I'm not feeling that great today; my throat is sore where I had the tube down there during the surgery. My drain is filling up and getting pretty heavy, so it pulls on the wound and also makes it difficult for me to get comfortable. I have to take off my main dressing today and I'm worried about that hurting. Keith has come up with a plan; first, I have to take a shower in the hope that might loosen the dressing, then, I must sit on the bed to remove the dressing in case I faint!

Later – the plan worked and I feel much better! I had the shower, but only with Keith's help. He has bought me a lovely natural sponge and we used that to wash my hair and soak the dressing. Then I lay on the bed and between us we worked the dressing loose and eventually got it off. Keith cried a bit, as he said just a few weeks ago I was a lively, healthy person, full of life and now I'm an invalid with probably worse to come. Amy came over and brought Lilli with some flowers and a penguin for me! Lilli was so careful with me, I covered up my drain as Amy is squeamish and I didn't want Lilli to be upset.

Mum has been to see me, my brother fetched her around yesterday. She was very quiet and neither of us mentioned her appalling behaviour. I think if she tried to justify it, I would find it hard to listen. It is her birthday tomorrow and as I won't be able to spend it with her, we have bought some cake and soft drinks for all the residents. Keith will take it around for after lunch.

Saturday, 16 January

Ellie came home last night. She wanted to come when I was in hospital, but I asked all the girls to wait until I felt ready. When she arrived, we had a big hug and sat up until gone 10.30, chatting. It was so lovely to have her here. Today, I had to go and have my drain taken out. It was below freezing, so I wrapped up well for the short journey back to the breast unit. I put on my soft bra with my little cushion inside, it still feels strange to only have one breast. I wore baggy clothes that would disguise my loss! The nurse took my drain out very quickly. It made me feel a bit queasy as I felt it slide up and out of my chest.

Sunday, 17 January

All three of the girls have been here together today, so now I'm tired and need an early night. They wanted to ask questions about the surgery and also about what happens next. I told them that when I was diagnosed, it was made clear that I would probably need chemotherapy plus radiotherapy and also hormone therapy. This is because of the type of cancer I have. I was worried about Ellie as she is my natural daughter and having a mother and grandmother both of whom have had cancer may have put her at a higher risk – but this isn't the case. My cancer and my mum's are different and neither is hereditary. This was a relief.

We also talked about the fact that until I have a CT scan, we cannot rule out that the cancer has already moved somewhere else and that I might have secondary cancer already. It was found in the lymph nodes, but this could either be a good or a bad thing. They could have been doing a good job of gathering up the cancer cells and stopping them going anywhere else, or it could suggest that the tumour had already metastasised. The CT scan and results will be a huge milestone for me but it won't happen until my wound has healed and I am recovered enough to attend an appointment. I know I have to get well as soon as possible and to do that I had to give in and sleep and try and lead a stress-free life!

18th January 2016 10.02

So it has been a week since my op… hard to believe. I have been very lucky; no real pain and my arm isn't stiff, so I have been able to wash my own hair and wear ordinary clothes.

All three girls have visited me over the weekend. Ellie came up from Kent on Friday after work and stayed until today. It has been lovely to have her here to talk to and she has visited Mum every day. She also bought me loads of Agatha Christie's to read plus DVDs to watch, including *Game of Thrones* and *Mad Men*! I'm saving those for later in my treatment.

Amy dropped in with Lilli on Thursday for a short visit, bringing me a penguin chosen for me by Lilli! She was very good and careful with me. Then on Saturday evening, Emma, Stan and Billy drove up. Billy is such a smiley, little boy… absolutely full of life. We all ended up here together on Sunday morning. It was busy but wonderful to see them all and to talk things over. Emma had got up to make a snowman with Lilli, so everyone was already excited.

My brother came up earlier in the week and drove Mum around to see me. He goes back out to Tenerife this week for the next two months. Yet, again we missed our week in the sun… We had to cancel as we were booked to be there last week! Mum is still worried, but all of the girls have visited her this weekend as I really don't feel able. She is quite confused about what has gone on which makes her exhausting to deal with.

On Thursday I had to take off my dressing. I was worried as it was so well stuck, but Keith and I managed it and I could see the full impact of the op. It is very neat. I have quite a bit of numbness around my armpit due to nerve damage, but as I've said, no pain. Then on Saturday, Keith took me to hospital to have my drain taken out. It wasn't very nice but at least I no longer have to drag a full bottle of gunk around with me. It was as big as a milk carton and basically full by the time it came off! Keith bent down to give me a kiss the other day, leant on the tube and almost did me a permanent injury!!! So now 'I'm free'! As you can hear, Keith is in this with me all the way!!!

I have enjoyed watching the spacewalk this week. Seems strange that this is going on above our heads. I am now sleeping better due to the lack of the drain but I have lots of strange dreams! Keith also has vivid dreams so we compare notes! I sometimes get tired during the day and have a nap, but some days I know I won't sleep so don't bother trying. Since I retired, I haven't slept that well and am used to managing on just a few hours.

So now it's just about healing. Then we have a big week in February when I go back to see my consultant to find out what the lymph nodes have told them and what my treatment plan is. I guess it won't be that pleasant but I really just want to get on with it – I do love a plan!!!!! At about the same time Mum has her appointment with her consultant. Ellie is coming up then to help me with that.

Thanks to everyone for my cards and flowers! We have run out of vases! Thanks also for all your messages and thoughts. I do enjoy reading them. I keep having to add names to my e-mail list, as different people get in touch. As always if you want to forward my e-mail on to anyone, feel free – none of this is a secret!

I will be in touch again soon.

Pam xxxx
Sent from my iPad

Tuesday, 19 January

Couldn't sleep last night as I was in lots of pain. My chest is much bruised and it's all coming out now. I needed to take some heavy-duty painkillers and get to bed early.

Thursday, 21 January

I am feeling a bit better; I have slept a lot and thought a lot and got on with getting better! Good news today; Mum's house has been sold, so we don't have to worry about that standing empty anymore. It's sad that I won't go there again,

I had a great childhood. I often wonder how Dad would have coped with me having cancer – I was his 'little girl' and he would have hated to see me hurt in anyway. Perhaps it's a good thing he died before this happened.

Sunday, 24 January

Keith went out last night without me. We have talked this over and decided that he must have a life while I'm ill or as much of a life as we can manage. We have always done things separately as well as together and we mustn't just cling to each other now. I'm thinking that if the worse did happen and I died, I don't want Keith to have lost contact with his friends and have a yawning gap.

The girls have all been doing their bit by visiting Mum when possible. Also, others are also helping, including my nephew who drove up to see us both. I have seen some of my close friends but I'm too tired for too many visitors and my plan is to reserve my energy for the next stage.

Tuesday, 26 January

I had to give in and go to the seroma clinic today to get my breast drained. As I've always had big breasts, my body is trying to fill up the space with liquid. It is painful as the pressure builds up. My nurse was very gentle and I didn't feel a thing, partly due to the fact that I have some parts of my body that are now permanently numb – I guess this is due to nerve damage caused by surgery.

Wednesday, 27 January

I was awake and up again at 2.30 a.m. I'm finding it impossible to get a good night's sleep and I guess that is probably a long way off.

Later – Marie came for me today and we went out for coffee. I had spent a good couple of hours trying on clothes with my cushion in! It looked OK. I felt good and enjoyed being out doing ordinary things.

Thursday, 28 January

A lovely day to remember! Ellie was here for her friend's wedding. It was taking place locally, so I was able to go down to see the bride and her attendants arrive. Ellie, was a bridesmaid and looked so lovely and happy. We had our photo taken together, I tried not to think dark thoughts about this being a photo to treasure if I died, but even in the middle of something so lovely, these things still pop up into my mind. I didn't need to sleep, even though I had been out for a long time on a cold day.

Monday, 1 February

Ellie and I took Mum to her appointment at the breast clinic – something I really didn't want to do. I didn't want to go back to clinic again but I had to. It was good news for Mum; her tumour was responding well to her medication. Ellie was wonderful with Mum, reading magazines to her and keeping her well entertained.

Tuesday, 2 February

I have my check up on Thursday but I've just opened a hospital letter telling me about my appointment with an oncologist at the Royal. This letter pre-empts my meeting on Thursday, I now know that my plan includes chemotherapy. I feel very low; it smashes the small hope I had that I wouldn't need chemo. I'm very scared that I won't be able to cope with it. I have heard that it is pretty brutal.

Thursday, 4 February

Chemo is confirmed, as are radiotherapy and hormone therapy. I'm to have it all. I have a date for my CT scan as well. I have moved on to the next part of my journey – this journey I would rather not be on. I have a new consultant for this who I will meet soon. I feel bereft saying 'Goodbye' to my surgeon who I have trusted with my life.

Chapter 8
The Lull Before the Storm

Last night I dreamt of Dad. I know it was a dream, but it was comforting; he put his arm around me and spoke to me and I felt safe and hopeful. Today we go to see my oncologist and hear the results of my CT scan. This is such an important day. If I have secondary cancer, there is no cure and I have to react to that. We are ready, waiting to go and both of us feel terribly sick.

Later, we waited in a busy waiting room at oncology. There were women there in all different stages of treatment, some with no hair and wearing hats or wigs. I will have to think about how I will deal with that, what I will do. When we were called in, our consultant had no CT results for me! There had been a mix up and delay – she wasn't best pleased! We had to go away for a while and then go back. I had been angry at first, but now I was drained and just feeling scared. On our return, we were shown straight into the consulting room. I felt scared walking past everyone who was waiting, I wanted to say, "No, let all of these people go first, I'll wait." In that way, I would have a few more minutes or hours without terminal cancer, but we were escorted in, there was no avoiding the truth. In the room I tried not to look at the doctor; I didn't want to see bad news in her eyes. She put her arm around me and told me that my scan was good, it was clear, I didn't have cancer anywhere else; in fact, I didn't have cancer anymore! Keith and I ran off to have lunch to celebrate and we rang the girls so that they could celebrate too.

17 February 2016 11.39

Just wanted to update everyone. I've had busy times at the hospital! First, I met my consultant oncologist who seems pretty good. The same afternoon, I was back in an ambulance with Mum to A&E as she had fallen and needed X-rays. We spent over 5 hours there when they finally decided to admit her… she eventually got on a ward at midnight!!! It was all horrible. The next day, she was discharged and waited four hours for an ambulance home. I couldn't stand it any longer, so Keith and I went and rescued her at about 7.30 p.m. so that she could sleep in her own bed. It seems she may have broken a small bone in her hip – she will have a CT scan next week!

Talking of CT scans… I have also had the pleasure of having one of them myself this week! Quite a strange experience when they inject the liquid that will help highlight what they're looking for. However, at least it's quick.

I will now start my chemo next week. I am glad to have a few days rest before the first session as I do feel pretty tired from worrying about the scan results. Ellie is coming this weekend, so I can enjoy her company too.

I have no idea how my body will react to the chemo. I have it one day in week, then I get two weeks to recover. I'm really hoping that I can have 'normal' days. Each person is different, so I will have to wait and see. There are quite a lot of unpleasant side effects, so I'm hoping I don't get them all! I have to be really careful that I don't get any infections as my immune system will be low. If you are thinking of visiting me, please don't come if you have anything I could catch!

I will be in touch again soon when I can say some more. Keith and I are going to a meeting about the chemo this Saturday so that should answer any questions we have. I am also going to a couple of workshops about hair loss and how to look after myself during my treatment.

Pam x

Sent from my iPad

Wednesday, 17 February

After the excitement of hearing the CT scan was clear, we were dropped back into despair with a phone call saying Mum was yet again on the floor at her flat and an ambulance had been sent for. At least this time she had been found quickly, not like last time when she was on the floor for hours as she had forgotten about the emergency cord in her bathroom! This time I rushed over and found myself in A&E again. She was admitted in the early hours. It is obvious that some investigation needs to take place before she is sent home again, otherwise nothing will have changed and she will be admitted again and again and again. I need to be strong and assertive if I can find the energy.

Later, after talking very strongly to the consultant on the ward, it was agreed that there must be some underlying reason for Mum falling so often and that this needs investigating.

Saturday, 20 February

We went on a pre-chemo visit to the chemo suite today... only problem was that we couldn't go in as it was being decorated! We looked through a glass panel in the door at a room covered in sheets, very illuminating! We were given a talk by the nurse in charge. There were about 12 of us there with partners or friends. I had been thinking about whether I want to try the cold cap. This may help to save my hair, but it means going in at least two hours before my appointment and also stopping at the suite for at least an hour after the chemo is finished. To be honest, I don't want to spend any more time in hospital than I have to. I just want to get on with it and then get away. Also, there's no guarantee it will work. I can understand why young women might want to do it; it worked well for my friend's daughter, but I really can't be bothered. Our talk was pretty frightening in places; however, Keith and I got the giggles because our nurse kept referring to catastrophic incidents'. She didn't explain what these might be, but if one happened, then partners and other patients had to 'get out of the way'! Hopefully, we won't have one of those as I'm not sure we would recognise it if we saw it coming! After the talk, we went to visit Mum and found she had been moved to another ward! We went to check what was going on and to insist she wasn't discharged until properly ready.

Wednesday, 24 February

Today I spent part of the day at a make-up session called 'Look Good Feel Better'. It was put on for women who have breast cancer. They taught us how to make the most of ourselves, and particularly, how to draw on eyebrows if you lose them. I enjoyed it so much, as I got a chance to talk to other women in the same boat as me. Some were further on and had lost their hair, but they looked well and we had a laugh which I wasn't expecting.

Afterwards, I went up to the ward to see Mum. Ellie was visiting, so we all had sandwiches together. The hospital has found that Mum did break a bone from an earlier fall, but the treatment is to weight bear in controlled circumstances. They are going to move her to a community hospital to ensure she is ready when she is discharged. I need her to be well while I'm having my chemo.

My friend, who has had the same chemo as me, brought me a survival kit; so thoughtful. It had sugar free sweets for when my mouth tastes awful, a new toothbrush and toothpaste, as I have to clean my teeth after I eat or drink anything to stop any infections. It also contained non-scented shower gel, plus a large tub of E45 for when I have radiotherapy. She also bought me a selection of hats and a wig. She told me that I have to be selfish and look after myself. This is so difficult when Mum needs me. After she had gone, I tried the wig on – I'd also got another from a different friend. Ellie was here and she tried them on too and then we got Keith into one – we did laugh! We felt a bit guilty, but I'm sure that both my friends would love to know they'd given me an hour of fun.

This evening, Keith and I went to see Mum for the last 45 minutes of visiting time. I'm not sure when I will be able to *visit again. I can't risk getting an infection once I've had the chemo, because as well as destroying any cancer cells, it will kill off my immune system, so getting an infection would be dangerous. I won't be able to go to see her in the hospital. I also won't be able to see my grandchildren if there's any chance of me catching anything.*

I have tried to rest before my chemo but that hasn't really happened in the way I'd hoped. My first session is tomorrow; I know it will be hard, but I know I can be strong and that I'll get loads of backup from Keith and my family. Keith has refurbished our bedroom to make it cosier and bright; it was looking a bit jaded. He said that if I have to spend time in there, it needs to be comfortable. What a lucky woman I am to have someone so thoughtful on my side. I will try and sleep tonight by thinking of lovely things.

Chapter 9
Fecking Chemo

I've had my first chemo. We started the day slowly as my appointment was at 2.30, so we had plenty of time to wait. We went for a walk in the sun and ate our main meal at lunchtime as we didn't know how long we would be at the hospital. We also made a sandwich and left it in the fridge, ready to come home to. We were covering all bases! We had to wait over two and a half hours in the waiting room as they were running late. Then I was taken through.

The suite was very basic; there was no privacy. Beds and chairs were quite close together, all full of patients. I was to attend this suite every three weeks for six sessions. There was a fridge with sandwiches for patients but not companions, diluted orange was available and so was fruit.

I chose to sit on a chair and a lovely nurse, called Betty, came to do my treatment. Keith had nowhere to sit as Betty had to sit up close to me. I was put on a drip and then over the course of about 45 minutes, Betty added three syringes of different chemicals through a cannula on the top of my hand. She pushed these in gently and slowly, chatting away. Then when she'd completed that, she gave us a 'home kit'. This included anti-nausea drugs and a series of steroid injections. Keith and I were shocked – this hadn't been mentioned to us. I told Betty that I didn't need them, thinking that she would check my notes and say she'd made a mistake, but no, she checked my notes and confirmed I had to have one a day for five days! I was horrified at the thought of injecting myself – I have to turn away when watching Holby City! Keith stepped in and said that he could do them for me, so we left with a lovely parcel to take home. It was all pretty surreal and no catastrophic incidents! Now I'm home, I feel a bit lightheaded, sick and quite tired, so I'm planning an early night.

Friday, 26 February

I felt very sick last night but I wasn't so – that's good. Today I've felt tired, so I've stayed in my fluffy dressing gown and done very little. I've eaten as usual, perhaps I'm going to be OK with this chemo. It is called FEC, but Keith and I call it fecking chemo!

29th February 2016 12.01

So last Thursday, I went for my first chemo. We arrived at oncology with a bag of things to keep me busy… Knitting, reading etc., as I didn't know how long it would take. Unfortunately, they were understaffed and running one and a half hours late when we arrived! So we sat in the waiting room, glad of our books etc. We actually got in over two hours late, but then it was all systems go. I was on a drip and then my chemo was added by a nurse who sat with me all the time. 3 different chemicals – the first very pink, almost like a cocktail. Well, I suppose that's what the whole thing was…… A poisonous cocktail. Luckily, it only took 45 mins and we were allowed to go home so we were back here early evening. I felt OK until about 8, then went to bed feeling pretty sick.

Friday was a bumpy day. I wasn't sick, but felt pretty nauseous and sometimes tired. By Saturday and Sunday, I really felt exhausted and didn't know what to do with myself. Keith kept me drinking regularly and tempted me with food… Little but regular. When I wasn't actually asleep, I found it impossible to concentrate on anything for long, so I had to give in.

Today was something I'd been dreading. For the next 5 days, I have to have an injection into my stomach under the skin… oh and it's DIY… you're expected to do it yourself!!!

I hate injections! I knew I couldn't do it but Keith thought he could. There were no instructions on the box and unsurprisingly neither of us could remember what the nurse had told us! So Keith looked it up on the internet, you can find out how to do anything if needed! So we've done that now. He was so gentle. We had big cuddles afterwards and quite a few tears. So far today I feel better, so that's why I'm writing this e-mail... while I have the energy. I am hoping I am getting past the worst bit of this cycle but can't be sure how I will feel later today, let alone tomorrow.

I haven't been able to visit Mum (Keith is also doing all of that too. Amy is fixing to go one evening to give him a break. She and Ellie visited when Mum was in the main Leicester hospital – that was horrible, as Mum was very confused and in lots of pain). Mum is now in a community hospital about five miles away. She did break a small bone in her hip when she fell and we have had to fight to get her the support she needs, but Keith tells me she is so much better that it was worth it.

I am not up to visitors at the moment. I would find it too draining. I do hope to see some of you soon though, when this first part of the cycle is over. Thanks for your messages – I always read them. As always please pass my news on to anyone who you think would like to know how it's going.

Pam x
Sent from my iPad

Monday, 29 February

Things have gone downhill fast. On Sunday I had backache and I felt very tired, but I was still eating; this doesn't surprise me – our family are great eaters. Even when we're ill, we eat – I learnt this from Mum and Dad. Last night I hardly slept, my mind was drifting all over the place, darting from one thing to another. I tried to settle it by thinking about holidays in the past, but I couldn't contain it at all. Today I had my first steroid injection. Keith looked up on the internet the best way to do it! God bless the internet. I lay on the bed gripping my tummy to make a roll of fat (not too dif-

ficult), and then he did it. We were both scared and cried afterwards, four more to go.

Tuesday, 1 March

I feel desperate, cold and frightened. I can't drink enough to get these toxins through me. I have to clean my teeth after I've eaten or drunk anything to avoid infection in my gums which are a danger area. I find the taste of toothpaste nauseous and then I try to drink but can't do it. When I wee, it smells of the chemo and is bright pink, which scared me the first time I saw it – nobody told me it would be the same colour as the chemicals. The smell is awful and I feel it is also coming out of my pores. I'm scared I won't be strong enough and will give up and stop having treatment. Keith tells me that will never happen.

Wednesday, 2 March

I'm proud of myself; I made a plan and it is working. I decided to use baby toothpaste which has a sweetish taste, when I do that my mouth feels better and I can drink the large quantities of water I need to work the chemo through my system. I've also tried drinking hot water, a friend of mine does this instead of tea and I suddenly remembered her. Hot water is better for me. I keep a flask by my bed, for during the night, I keep drinking whenever I'm awake. Of course, that means I have to get up and wee more, but I feel that this is good as it is cleansing me. When I wake up in the morning, I'm starving, so I now take some snacks up with me to eat as soon as I wake up; this gives me some energy. I know that I'm past the worse, but I'm tired by it all, so I'm looking after myself by not seeing anyone. I get up in the morning, then go back to sleep in the afternoon. When I sleep, I dream lots; strange dreams, but not unpleasant. I have to build up my strength ready for the next session, I want to stay on track. I've heard that if you can, you should stay on track, as this allows the best chance for the chemo to do its job. If I have to go through this, I want it to bloody well work!

Thursday, 3 March

I cried yesterday because a friend e-mailed me and told me she was going to be spending Mother's Day with her daughter and go to Betty's in Harrogate for afternoon tea. It was a lovely e-mail, full of news, but it made me so jealous. I wanted to go to Betty's and eat Yorkshire fat rascals with my daughter. Instead, I was going to be stuck here while she was in Kent working all weekend. I could feel myself using that phrase that I hated when I was a teacher, "It's not fair!" I managed to e-mail her back without saying those words and wished her a lovely time and I did say I envied her. Today, I received a parcel from Betty's with two fat rascals and some scones! Keith and I have wolfed them down. I enjoyed mine so much; the first thing that has taken the taste of chemo out of my mouth. Thank you, dear friend.

I also received some liquorice pipes today! From a friend that I worked with who loved liquorice almost as much as me. When I was on interview for the job and feeling quite nervous, he and I had had a conversation about the liquorice fields around Pontefract – he was amazed that I had worked at the liquorice factory in Sheffield where I had put the glowing embers on the pipes by hand! Once Betty's cakes were gone, I started in on the pipes!

Sunday, 6 March – Mothers' Day

Still not sleeping very well, many of my dreams are 'blasts from the past'. The other night I got up and listened to the whole of Tapestry by Carole King – I found it on the internet. It reminded me of being at college. I was the only person on my corridor to have a stereo system. My dad bought it for me before I went – he said it was made in Siberia by Russian prisoners in gulags. Could this have been true? My brother chipped in and bought me a James Taylor album and off I went to Sheffield. Later I got the Tapestry LP and played it continuously. I used to leave my door open so that everyone could listen. As I had music, my room was a bit of a magnet, a meeting place. I was also very popular as my parents used to come and see me regularly, bringing food parcels. After they'd gone, friends would arrive to help me unpack the box, usually there would be cider and biscuits and cakes plus sweets. What high living!

Today Keith and I went to see Mum, she was back at Oak Court having graduated with honours from the community hospital, having managed to get up and dressed and make her way to the dining room for breakfast every day. I was anxious about how Mum would be, but she looked well. We hugged and I started to cry. Mum said, "Stop this, you're doing so well."

Friday, 11 March

I was quite shocked earlier this week when I was out with a good, friend and my hair started to fall out. I thought it wouldn't do that until after my second session, not sure why I thought that though. It is definitely going. We were sitting having coffee when it felt like someone had opened the back door and a cold draught cut across the room. I shivered and pulled my cardigan around me tighter – as I did this, I noticed something drifting across the table. I went to brush it away only to find it was a neat tuft of my hair! I prayed that it wouldn't all just drop out onto the table in one fell swoop. I want to go out tomorrow night and I want to still have hair. We are going to one of the places we usually go to once a month to dance. I still feel a bit tired but will dance a bit. I have decided to spray my hair within an inch of its life in the hope that it acts like glue and keeps it on my scalp. The last thing I want is to dance vigorously and find it falling out over the dancefloor.

My hair has gone! I put my plan into action and my hair looked OK – a bit like a very drastic cut! Then this morning I decided to shower and basically it looked like I had a rat in the cubicle with me. All that was left on my scalp was a few long strands – this was not attractive. I let Keith shave my head and got my hats out and chose one to wear tomorrow. I feel remarkably 'unbothered'. I'm not defined by my looks; I'm defined by the way I am and how I act.

Tomorrow I have a blood test at my GP's. Then on Tuesday I see my oncologist who will tell me whether I can continue with my next chemo treatment on Thursday, I want to stay on track.

16 March 2016 17.44

Just wanted to let everyone know that Keith and I saw the oncologist yesterday. Although my blood hasn't fully recovered from my first lot of chemo, they are going ahead with my second cycle tomorrow. This means following treatment on Thursday, I will probably have 5 or 6 rough days. To help me recover ready for the third cycle, they want me to have injections for 8 days instead of just 5! Whoopee! Keith can't wait! Luckily, he is so good at it that I'm ok about it.

Also, I am now officially without my hair. I managed to hold on to most of it to go out on Saturday night. I knew it was going to be my best chance of getting a night out dancing and we managed it 'cos I was feeling pretty good apart from a tickly cough. So we made it to one of our favourite places in Nottinghamshire where we met up with lots of friends who we haven't seen for ages. It was great! Then on Sunday my hair paid the price. Whilst showering, it basically all fell out apart from a few long strands. It was not at all attractive, so Keith shaved it all off for me. I am now sporting a collection of hats! To be honest, I'm really surprised that I don't care. I thought when it came to reality, I might feel different, but I really don't care. I have been out to the village shopping and also to Slimming World, which was harder 'cos everyone takes their hats off inside except me, but it's just part of how it is for me at the moment.

My granddaughter came yesterday. It took her over an hour to ask what I had on my head and why. I told her I have to take very important medicine but it has made my hair disappear. Obviously, she wanted to look… She is almost three and incredibly curious. So I took my hat off. She stroked my head and then massaged it very gently, saying, "I will magic it back." She was a bit disappointed it didn't work but moved on to something else. Today she told her daddy that nanny looked 'lovely' without hair! What a cutie!

So you won't hear from me for a while, but I will return! Remember, no news is good news for a few days.

Pam x

Chapter 10
More Fecking Chemo

Thursday, 24 March

Ellie has been here, but it was dreadful because I felt so ill. This time around, I started off getting on better, then I got a terrible sore throat that made me feel so wretched. I have hardly had the energy to even talk to Ellie, let alone do anything nice. She has visited nanny and sorted a few things out there. She found out that one of the other residents has passed on some tablets to Mum which she made Mum give back. We can do without Mum taking unknown medications, she messes up her own sometimes, taking things at the wrong time of the day, and this is partly why she has fallen in the past. I have decided that Ellie and the other girls can't come at the beginning of my cycle; I don't want them to see me like this. I don't want anyone to see me in such despair. It's not just the awful symptoms: the sores around my lips which crack and bleed when I talk, the continuous ache in my back, the constipation, it's the psychological state of me. Sometimes I really want to give in and just let the bloody cancer do its worst.

There are times when I ask myself and Keith whether this is worth it. I know it is, but sometimes, I just lose sight of that for a while.

Saturday, 26 March

During the early hours of this morning, I woke to find my temperature rising. If it goes above a certain point, this could mean that I have an infection, so I have to ring in to the oncology department. So I had to stay awake to keep checking. I also had my sore throat back and my gums hurt. I really don't want to have to go into the hospital, and I certainly don't want to be admitted to the ward – that is what all of us try to avoid. I drank loads of water and took paracetamol, and luckily, my temperature came down.

Tuesday, 29 March

Amazingly, Keith and I made it to London at the weekend and managed the theatre and a meal out, something I really didn't think I would do. Keith had planned it well so that I got time for a sleep before we went out. I was so grateful for all the thought that went into it. This is a golden memory in a grey time – I need more of them.

29 March 2016 15.25

I think it is about time I wrote to you all.

I have just returned from a trip to London! I really didn't think I would be doing anything like this, but we managed it. Keith had booked this before Xmas and we kept it in the diary in the hope we could go and it turned out, we were right to do that. So yesterday Keith drove us down to a hotel, so that I could have a rest in the afternoon. After that, we got a taxi into theatre land and had a meal together, before going to see Lazy Sunday Afternoon, the story of the Kinks. It was a good show and we really enjoyed it. We got a taxi back and I fell into bed. Then this morning we had a lovely breakfast and made our way back. It was so great to do this together after a difficult second chemo cycle.

Yes, the 2nd cycle was very hard. I managed to suffer some new symptoms, as well as the ones I'd had first time around. Ellie was here on what turned out to be my worst day. It was hard for us both, for her to see me so wretched. However, it did pass and I just have to remember that when I'm in the middle of it.

I know several of you want to meet up with me. I do want to see people, but I only really get one week in 3 when I have much time. The week after chemo is taken up with feeling awful and trying to rest to pull out of it. The week before chemo I have to have blood tests and my appointment with my oncologist, so my time is already being eaten up. (This time around I also have to go for an Echocardiogram to check out my heart before a change in my chemo and further treatment.) That means I have one full week to do things with Keith, see my mum, do things with the girls and our grandchildren etc. As you can imagine, even in my good times, I still need to be careful not to do too much each day as I need my blood counts to recover, otherwise my chemo will be delayed which we don't want. So if you haven't seen me, please bear with me.

I am going to send you another e-mail with a photo of me, taken on the morning of my last chemo. I had dressed and applied full make up. Now that I have no hair, I can spend more time on lashings of mascara! We were going out for lunch prior to going to the hospital for me to be poisoned again!!! I am quite used to having no hair now and am very happy with my hats. While I still have lashes and eyebrows, I am making the most of them!

So, hopefully, I will get to see some of you soonish.

Pam xxx

Sent from my iPad

5 April 2016 15.01

I have just had a lovely week!

Since returning from London, I have been shopping in town, plus out dancing where we saw loads of our friends. Friends are great; they give us lots of encouragement and strength. Then on Sunday night, I was
well enough to enjoy cooking for us; Ellie and Emma and Keith. I had lots and lots of cuddles with Billy and the girls. They have all gone now. I'm exhausted but so happy.

This morning, Keith and I have been to see the oncologist who says my blood is 'perfect'. So I get my third lot of chemo on Thursday afternoon. I don't want it but am glad I am on track as this means, as a family, we will be able to go to the Cotswolds for a long weekend later this month. Ellie and Keith organised it before I was diagnosed and we have really hoped we could all make it and now it looks like we will!

So another poisoning on Thursday with some horrible side effects, but then I will be half way through! Whoopee! Can't wait!

I still have eyelashes and eyebrows, so hoping they're here to stay! Lilli 'lays her hands' on my head every time she comes, so eventually when I get my hair back, she will believe she 'magicked it'!

So I will be in touch after the next cycle. Keep telling me your news... I love it.

Pam x

Sent from my iPad

27 April 2016 12.46

Dear all, I wanted to tell you how things have been recently. We made it to the Cotswolds. Keith n I drove down via Moreton in The Marsh. The house was lovely, perfect for all of us, and in a beautiful setting. Everyone arrived by Thursday eve... Billy slept in his PJs taken straight up to bed, closely followed by Lilli going off to her single bedroom. We all chatted and had a drink. I was later to bed than usual. It seems though, I was oblivious, Ellie and Andy stopped up to have another rum and at 2 a.m. In the morning, Amy found them having an emotional heart to heart! Amy broke up the party. The facilities were good and the big kids and little kids went swimming every day. I'm not allowed to swim in case I get an infection, so I had to just watch the fun. They also played football. Keith and I were having a very leisurely walk when we heard this mighty cheer from the other side of the estate; we realised our lot were cheering cos Lilli had scored a goal!!! They also went on bike rides with a baby seat and trailer so they could accommodate children who fall asleep! We girls all had our treatment at the spa which was lovely. As I've been told not to have a massage, I had purple sparkly nails – why have something ordinary???

It was lovely to see them together, sharing the childcare and getting on so well. We are so lucky. Although I felt fine and was sleeping at night, I was obviously asking too much of myself cos suddenly on Saturday afternoon, I felt very cold and tired and went to bed. I couldn't get up for the next 18 hours. When I did get up, we decided to drive home where I promptly went to bed.

I was worried that I had ruined my chances of staying on track. On Monday I had to go to the hospital for a blood test. It was so busy I had to wait one and a half hours. It was very draining. On Tuesday, we saw the oncologist who said my blood was fine and that I can go ahead tomorrow. I'm pleased I'm on track but I'm anxious as I still feel tired. I will be having Docetaxel or Taxotere. It's the one I haven't had yet, so we have no idea how I will respond.

So after tomorrow you probably won't hear from me for a while. When Keith gives me my injections, I look the other way and try to think of nice things. So I have lots of new pictures to draw on from our Cotswold trip; Lilli n Billy splashing each other encouraged by Stan and Andy! Ellie jumping into the outdoor Eco pool, another name for very cold and a bit dirty! Everyone swimming in the outdoor heated pool with steam rising – including Keith! Everyone spending at least half an hour at a time on the floor crawling with Billy who is so fast, especially if he spots a wire to pull! Ellie's face after her deep tissue massage which included the use of elbows!

I will be in touch at some point to tell you how things go. I'm hoping for a few fewer side effects, this time around, I seem to have had everything apart from being sick. Even so, Keith and I have had to curtail our meal choices radically, as I find it impossible to eat proper meat at any time and at some points in the cycle, I can only cope with very bland things. Keith has also gone off some things which is a bit strange, but I think it is due to association somehow. Also he won't eat things in the house that I wouldn't like the smell of. My sense of smell does seem heightened and some smells just make me gag! Not very polite in company!!!

Anyway, I must stop and send this; I have some jobs I must do today. Otherwise, once I've had chemo, I never know when I will have the strength. Talk again soon.

Pam xxx

Chapter 11
Anyone for T

Sunday, 1 May – Dad's Birthday

I slept badly last night; I had a temperature and my back was aching badly. I realised that my tongue was also swollen and in the night when I wasn't rational, I was afraid it would keep swelling and block my throat and air supply. So I sat up and eventually got out of bed. I have some thrush tablets that Keith fetched from the chemist, so I've had one of those and I'm trying to suck an ice cube.

Have heard from a friend in Northampton who has been ill with MS; she now has cancer and it is secondary, so there is no cure. She has sent me a message and I can feel the pain in it. I don't even have the energy to phone her today, let alone go and visit. I feel I'm letting her down.

Tuesday, 3 May

I'm still in pain with my back and I still have thrush. I haven't slept properly for so long now that I don't expect to. I got up early this morning to find out what had happened in the football yesterday; Leicester have won the Premier League Championship, such a fairy story, in some ways it gives me hope. Also, my former pupil Mark Selby has won the snooker world championship.

Thursday, 5 May

Yesterday turned into a nightmare. I felt dreadful and still had back pains, stomach-ache and I couldn't speak because of my tongue. Keith made the decision to phone in to oncology – I cried and begged him not to, as I was afraid of being admitted, totally irrational. I wanted to attend my friend's 60th birthday celebration and Lilli's birthday party at the weekend and couldn't see that staying safe was the priority. Luckily, Keith ignored my pleadings and made the call. They told us to come in so poor Keith had to get me into some clothes and into the car, we're not far from the hospital but it seemed to take an age. There were people out on the streets waving Leicester City flags to celebrate their success.

Once at the suite, they pumped me full of antibiotics and took bloods. I just wanted to lie on the floor but managed to stay upright in a chair. I felt like I could pass out at any moment. (Later I found out that 95% of my white cells had been destroyed which put me in real danger – thank goodness Keith insisted on taking me in.) I wasn't kept in, there were no beds vacant anyway. I was sent home later in the evening, clutching some medications that worked like a miracle on my symptoms.

I was stupid and was playing the stoic, being the strong woman. It was almost like playing a role and I played it too well. I have to learn from this.

10th May 2016 12.27

Hello everyone! It has taken me a while to e-mail you all. I'm afraid I had a really difficult 4th chemo cycle and am still a bit tired and poorly.

Not quite sure why though, as you know it was a different type of chemo. Also, I think Keith and I were a bit blasé and didn't realise things weren't going too well until a bit too late. Without going into too much detail, I had a lot of side effects that seemed to accelerate and by the time we had realised, I was so weak that Keith had to take me back into oncology for blood tests, anti-biotics and other medication. I didn't have to stay in, but it was abs awful. At one point, a very young nurse asked me on a scale of 1 to 10 how bad the pain in my mouth was. I replied 'ugh!' I really couldn't speak, eat or drink. After three attempts to get an answer, Keith translated for me, telling her he thought I was saying

10! Poor Keith was traumatised really at how quickly things happened. So it has taken us longer to recover. However, we are now starting to do a few things.

Luckily, the medication had started to take effect in time for me to go to my friend Marie's 60th birthday celebration for a couple of hours. We went to a meal at the Marriott. I was able to wear the dress I bought back before I started chemo when I wasn't sure if I would ever get to the shops again. I couldn't eat much cos I had ulcers all over my tongue... but the food I did have was abs delicious. After the food, Keith bought me home undressed me so I could go to bed and went back for the rest of the night. I didn't mind him going back I was so pleased to be there at all!

Then after resting most of the Sunday, we were also able to go to Lilli's party for a couple of hours... we even took my mum. It was that red-hot Sunday. Mum and I sat indoors and basically watched the kids having a great time. One minute, Lilli was in party clothes, the next she was dressed as the Little Mermaid, and then as a triceratops! She adores dressing up and also had a spider-man outfit – very fetching!

So Keith and I have learnt lessons, ready for my next chemo!

We don't really have any plans for the next week and a bit before chemo number 5 as we have decided to take one day at a time and be kind to ourselves.

In amongst being really poorly, I did realise that LCFC had triumphed and that Mark Selby had won the snooker... Great for Leicester. This week Ellie is in Budapest for a few days to celebrate a friend's birthday. Then next week she is hoping to get up here for the LCFC parade. She will then stay and is going to take me to my oncologist appointment to give Keith a morning off. We have decided, with regret, that we are not going to get down to Kent as planned early in June. After this bad experience, we have decided to concentrate on just getting to the end of my treatment and save Kent for after it is all over.

So we may be out and about a bit, but we may just have a bit of a quiet time to gather our strength. Whatever, I look forward to seeing you all soon and hearing your news.

Pam xxx
Sent from my iPad

18 May 2016 09.58

Just a quick e-mail to let you know that Ellie took me to see my oncologist yesterday. Despite still feeling a bit tired and having a strange cough that keeps me awake at night, my consultant says my blood is good so I can have my next chemo tomorrow. I also need to have my first hormone treatment injection. (Not looking forward to that!)

As I had such a poor experience last time, she is reducing the chemo dose a little and Keith will have to give me ten days of injections! Whoopee!

Ellie came home late on Sunday evening after work. Poor thing, she broke down in the middle lane leading into the Dartford Tunnel. Thank goodness, a Good Samaritan stopped and towed her into the side. Then she got going but didn't get home until about 2 a.m.! I was fast asleep!

As well as taking me to my appointment, she visited my mum who is very well at the moment. We also managed to have a lovely lunch out together. Ellie went to watch the LCFC parade and on to Victoria Park where she said it was incredible. A good time to visit.

So I have to admit, I'm not looking forward to tomorrow. I'm really hoping this cycle goes better as Keith and I are both pretty tired. I'm also thinking that after this one we only have one more to finish, which is wonderful. The end will really be in sight then.

So I'm having a quiet day today, just getting some jobs done before the chemo. It is Keith's b'day next Weds so I have had to get myself prepared for that in advance, by buying and wrapping his present and writing his card, as it will probably fall just after my worst days. We will have to celebrate after the event when I'm up to doing something.

I will e-mail again when I'm out the other side!

Pam x

31st May 2016 13.21

Just to let you all know I am recovering from chemo cycle 5. Thank goodness it was so much better than cycle 4, though it has still knocked me out! Thank goodness my oncologist dropped the dose so I at least felt I could 'cope'.

Keith has had a difficult time as he has had an awful pain in his shoulder that has continued for almost two weeks. I guess it is part physical and part stress. He found cycle 4 so difficult when I was so ill.

I made a decision not to try to do anything much between chemo 5 and six to just give myself a chance to rest. I have more or less stuck to that, but sometimes it makes the days very long. At times during the cycle, I find it impossible to read and physically I find it impossible to even walk around the block, let alone do anything else. So it is sometimes hard to fill the days. I have enjoyed watching the French Open as I love tennis...... well watching it!

I look forward to when this is over and I can feel fit again and start walking locally.

It was Keith's birthday last week. We had a lovely day. I had organised my present before I had chemo while I was able to shop online. On the day, our friends Marie and Dave bought us a homemade birthday cake which was yummy – luckily, I had more or less got rid of the thrush in my mouth, so I could eat sweet things again. Ellie and Emma were in touch and then Amy bought Lilli around for a short visit. She insisted on opening Keith's pressies and cards for him!

We also had some fabulous news. Amy and Andy are going to have another baby in November, a sibling for Lilli. We are thrilled and are already really looking forward to that!

So next Thursday I should have my last chemo. I cannot imagine how I will feel about that and then even more when I have got through the last awful days and start to recover. My oncologist will then plan my radiotherapy which is likely to be Monday to Friday every day for 3 weeks. I just want to get on with it and get it finished.

Hope everyone who did something at half term and/or bank holiday had a good time. Now we need some summer sun. I have bought some headscarves to protect my baldhead when it's sunny – I want to be able to use them! I think I have frightened the sun back in!

Pam x

17 June 2016 09.09

So it has been a week now since I had my last chemo! Today I am starting to feel human again.

I have found this cycle not only physically hard, but also psychologically difficult. Physically, I have had some of the usual symptoms, but as with each cycle some new things have turned up. My toenails and fingernails have felt like they were going to spontaneously combust. Keith could even feel the heat from the outside. I tried putting my finger ends in cold water but the contrast was too painful to bear. They are cooling now, but the beds have obviously been damaged, so my fingernails are either yellowy coloured and splitting, or bruised and ridged... the good thing is that they will re-cover.

Psychologically, I have given Keith quite a hard time. I suppose when you are going through something, you use all your energy on that. I have somehow found more time to think and that has made me weepier! With the rain outside and me inside, I'm surprised we haven't had the fire brigade around to pump us out!

Before I had my chemo, Keith and I managed a meal out to celebrate his birthday (late but miles better than never!). We shared tapas. We enjoyed the food and the slowness of it all – so relaxing. I also managed to go to a couple of hours of Andy's 40th birthday party which Amy held in the base-ment of a Leicester bar for him. It was the day after I had my chemo. I was pumped full of steroids and chemo so pretty hyper! I managed to stay on my feet for a while plus drink a Pimm's before falling into a taxi to go home! Worth it though!

So, next plans:

Go and see my mum as soon as I am recovered enough... Keith does a great job but I need to talk to her myself.

Next week we have an appointment with my new consultant who will give us details about my radiotherapy treatment plan; 3 weeks of short Monday to Friday sessions. Once we know when those are starting, we can have a plan of our own – I always need a plan!!!

Hopefully, I might get out of the house a bit, especially if the weather starts to be kinder!

So I might get to see some of you soon... that would be good.

Pam x

Chapter 12
Radio Ga Ga

Thursday, 23 June

Starting to do ordinary things more now, like today Keith and I walked to the polling station to cast our votes regarding the EU and whether we should exit. I've been worried by some of the anti-immigration campaigning which has verged on being racist. It particularly seemed important to vote, as last week Jo Cox, an M.P., was murdered, it looks like it was politically motivated. Her photo shows a lovely, young woman, a mother of two who was doing something she loved and felt strongly about. We need to stand up for democracy.

Sunday, 26 June

The country has voted to leave the E.U. I felt physically sick when I turned on the TV to hear the news. I am totally shocked and concerned that this will embolden racist groups and that won't be good for a city like Leicester. I'm quite ashamed that I have never been a political animal. I'm not sure why I haven't felt the need to protest and march as I care about my country and especially for the people in it who seem disenfranchised. I regret not taking up a friend's offer, years ago, to go to Greenham Common with her and her daughters. Recently, Ellie and I joined an anti-English Defence League march in the city. I was proud of myself, especially as it was freezing cold! We were shepherded about and didn't get close to the EDP which I was grateful for; I didn't want Ellie in danger at all.

Went to see Mum today, she was in a negative mood criticising others. I find it hard when she gets like this and wonder why she is this way.

Tuesday, 28 June

I've been to the hospital and I feel a bit low. It was good news at oncology where I was congratulated on finishing my chemo on time. Then I went to radiotherapy to get ready for that treatment. I had to have another CT scan and then tiny dots were tattooed on my body for lining up the machine; they will be permanent reminders. For something so small, it hurt when they did my right side. The good thing about my mastectomy site is that parts of it are still numb from nerve damage, so I didn't feel a thing on the left-hand side! I'm just a bit fed up with being tampered with. Everyone is gentle, but even so, I get moved about, touched, prodded, treated and again, I have no control.

Also, I still have a problem with not sleeping that is taking its toll. I haven't slept properly since I started treatment way back in January and during chemo it was particularly bad. I spent night after night awake, trying not to think depressing thoughts. I devised games to keep my mind off other things, I played Pointless on my own. I also spent lots of time naming things for every letter of the alphabet; flowers, food, cities etc.

I'm trying to sort out my sleep cycle by setting the alarm and getting up early, then trying to stay awake all day; no napping, but it's so hard. I've had sleeping tablets from my GP to help me set a pattern but we both feel I need to do this without them now. I am frightened of getting too tired to live though, or of getting ill due to tiredness – I have to be strong enough to manage the whole radiotherapy course, I can't fall at this hurdle.

Thursday, 30 June

I've had my Herceptin injection at home, the first of many. I have to have these hormones injected every 3 weeks for about a year. The nurse comes here to do it which is wonderful – not going into the hospital is definitely popular with me. The only problem is that the nurse has to stay with me for two hours in case I have an adverse reaction. Luckily, so far, I've been fine and we have a second sitting room so the nurse stays in there while I pretend she isn't here and get on with other things. The other great thing about the service is that I can have the injection anywhere in the country so I can go on holiday and still get treatment on time. Marvellous! My nurse was called Blessing and she is one!

Saturday, 2 July

It hardly seems possible that we are in July! Time is a strange thing when I was having chemo; each day seemed like an age and the nights were elastic as I waited for the rest of the world to wake up and join me. Now that I'm well enough to be doing things, time is, of course, flying and soon I will start my next treatment. Today I've been shopping with Ellie, we went in all her favourite shops and had lunch out together; it was amazing that I could do it. She is off to see Mum soon; hope she gets more out of her than I did yesterday. She was more interested in the TV than me! I'm having a quiet evening, otherwise I won't be able to get up tomorrow.

3 July 2016 08.56

Just wanted to let you all know that I don't start my radiotherapy until 25 July. Then I will have 3 weeks of treatment; Monday to Friday. We are now having a break! Keith and I are hoping to get a couple of days in Derbyshire... if we get two days of good weather!

This weekend Ellie has been home and we managed to have a day together with lunch and shopping! Today Emma and Billy plus Amy and Lilli are coming over for lunch. We have decided to make the most of our break by doing normal things. (Unfortunately, we also have a few medical appointments to fit in.)

I am feeling much better as the last of the chemo departs my body! My finger nails are still pretty painful and look horrible and my feet are a bit swollen and I still get tired if I do too much, but generally I can give most things a go now. I am hoping to swim soon… I am just trying to sort out my costumes with pockets for my prosthetic. There is a wonderful woman at the hospital who sews pockets for prosthetics in bras and costumes for a small fee which she donates to charity. The only problem is that as with most things at the hospital there is a waiting list! I am also sleeping much better, so all in all I am recovering.

Keith is also catching up with his sleep and starting to take up life again. Later this month, he and Dave are off for a spa day which I gave him for his birthday. He certainly deserves a relaxing day off! Mum is also well. We are looking forward to next weekend when my nephew, her grandson, and his family are coming up to have lunch with us. If the weather is good, they are going to bring a picnic for us all to eat at the park… such a lovely idea.

So you may see me out and about a bit more over the next few weeks.

Pam x
Sent from my iPad

Wednesday, 6 July

Yesterday, I went for a walk up to the church in old Blaby, so good to be out and about but such hard work. When I got to the church, I had to sit on the cold, front step for about 15 minutes to gather enough energy to make it home again. My feet are swollen and my soles are very sensitive. Will I be able to walk like I used to? I guess I will just have to wait and see. I've read that after chemo, some things may never recover and others will be right as rain. I really want my fingernails to get better. Yesterday I caught one on the car door and basically the whole thing came off, it was painful. I think they're going to get worse before they get better, looks like they are all going to fall off. Ugh!

Sunday, 10 July

Last week, Iris, an old friend of Mum's, came to visit her. My brother drove her over and she spent the day at Oak Court, sampling the delights of being looked after. I called in before they set off home, she seemed to have enjoyed herself and certainly approved of the place. Everyone should have the chance to live somewhere as nice when they need to, but sadly this isn't the case. It's always in the press and on the television about funding shortages for Social Care and also about awful nursing homes where the elderly are abused. I really feel for elderly people who have no one to look after them and 'stick up' for them. I don't look forward to being old but obviously I've been spending a lot of time lately trying to avoid the alternative! Mum and I watched the Wimbledon ladies' final together, I took Pimm's and two lovely cakes for us to enjoy. Keith and I went out on Saturday night to somewhere we haven't been for a while where we used to dance regularly. I felt anxious and realised that I feel less confident going out again as I don't want strangers to see me. I decided I had to go anyway; it wasn't a success. I tried to dance and realised how unfit I am – I couldn't even manage a short record.

Monday, 11 July

Steven and family came yesterday but were stuck on the motorway so arrived late. I rang Mum to let her know and she told me she had an upset tummy and didn't want to go out for a meal. This happens so often – I think she gets anxious about going out and this is how it manifests. Steven took it all in his stride and just called in at the local supermarket and bought a lovely picnic for us all. We ate it at Mum's, with the children sitting on the floor. Mum told us all that Angela Rippon is going to officially open Oak Court next week, she seems excited about meeting her which I'm surprised about.

Saturday, 16 July

We have managed a few days away in Derbyshire! Well it was one night and two days but it felt like a real holiday. We stayed at a large hotel which is famous for lovely food. We dressed to go into dinner. I wore the dress I'd had for Marie's birthday, with my orange and bright pink turban thingy. I felt great. We had four courses and half a bottle of champagne to celebrate actually being there. We went to Hathersage to see Little John's grave which Dad took me to as a child, we also had Bakewell puddings and bought Mum one for when we got back. It was wonderful to be doing 'real' things, not just hospital stuff. Keith cried a bit as he said I was so much better – it does feel like we are over the worse.

Thursday, 21 July

Summer has arrived, not a British summer... someone else's summer; it is 35 degrees here today! I love it during the day but find it too much at night. Last Monday, I went for my bone scan, it only took about ten minutes which I was glad about. I was worried when I got there and found that it was a young man working the scanner. I thought he might not have much empathy and that he would be rough with me. I felt ashamed afterwards for being so prejudiced, he was kind, thoughtful and so gentle.

Saturday, 23 July

I swam yesterday! I spent quite a lot of time at home in front of the mirror in my swimsuit checking out my profile. I looked at myself from every angle until I was sure I was satisfied no one could tell I was wearing a prosthetic. Luckily, at our gym there are two small changing rooms inside the women's communal changing area, so I can use one of those. I shower, then take off my suit and prosthetic, wrap myself up carefully in a big fluffy towel, then 'leg it' to the room. I don't want any children to see my flat chest and the scars, it might upset them. I don't mind about adults, they can cope. It was wonderful in the water, so relaxing, even though I pushed myself to see what I was capable of, I was very pleased.

Thursday, 28 July

I've had four days of radiotherapy. Keith took me on day one just in case I wouldn't be able to drive afterwards but I was fine. My team are so funny, they obviously get on well with each other and included me in their jokes. Once I was on the bed thing, everything got quiet and serious. They have to line up my tattoos perfectly, moving me just a matter of millimetres. The machine is massive, and at one point it transmitted blue beams across my body. Everything is double, if not triple checked, before they leave the room and the radiotherapy is switched on. I feel nothing except the urge to cough or sneeze just when I can't. It's all over in less than ten minutes then I grab a sweet from the counter before driving the five miles home. I'm lucky I live this close it must be exhausting if you have to travel in everyday just for ten minutes. If I'm really quick, I can beat the car park and get out without paying. This is another thing I think about, what do people do who can't afford it? We have bought a 'season ticket' which gives us half price parking but to do that you have to have the money to lay out in the first place.

28 July 2016 17.17

I have now started my radiotherapy. Three done so far this week, so just 12 sessions to go now! So far, I have had no side effects that I've noticed. I'm taking myself to the suite as it doesn't need two of us. The team and the machine are pretty amazing. It takes three people to set me up, they are so accurate.

In my ordinary life, I am doing more normal things. I am going swimming again and walking more. We managed to get to Derbyshire and walked on the Monsall Trail cos that is flat. We also walked in the grounds of Chatsworth in the sun. Our hotel bedroom was a bit tired but our four-course evening meal was delicious and the service was excellent.

Last week, some friends came from Norway to see us and Mum. We all had a lovely lunch together. We took them into Leicester to visit the Richard III centre and his tomb in the cathedral.

For his birthday (last May) I had given Keith a day at a spa for him and Dave. I wanted him to have some time away from me. They went last week and combined it with a soul night in Birmingham.

We now know Amy is having another girl due on 1st December… we are all so excited! Ellie is at her busiest at the lighthouse with loads of visitors but she is coming up to see me next week.

So just two weeks left and then most of my treatments will be over. We plan to book a holiday for September. Then we will have lots to look forward to, including a big birthday for Ellie in September, Billy's birthday in August, our holiday, a trip to Kent and to Ellie's lighthouse in October, my birthday in November and a new baby ready for Xmas! Things are looking up!

I still have no hair and only about six eyelashes and very sparse eyebrows. I would like it all to start growing now as I fancy having a hairstyle! My nails are a mess but apart from these small things and a few others, I'm myself again!

So I am gradually going to be getting back into doing more things. I will pick up my charity work in September, I'm looking forward to that. I should start to see everyone that I haven't seen for a while, so I'm making this my last update e-mail. Thanks again to everyone who has replied at any time and kept me going. Thanks to all of you for reading my e-mails and thinking of me (over 60 of you in the end!). I suppose I could have done it on my own but it would have been far lonelier and harder… knowing you were all there made a real difference.

Pam xxx Sent from my iPad

Monday, 15 August

Last Friday, I had my last radiotherapy session. Whoopee! I took sweets in for on reception, I've eaten a fair, few myself while attending appointments. I had a review a few days earlier, Keith and I were a bit disappointed as we were advised not to go abroad yet as my skin may react badly to the sun. I need to keep covered up for a while. We had planned to try and get a deal for Ibiza which we both love out of season when the crowds have gone. We will just have to wait a little longer. I went for my echocardiogram today to check the radiotherapy hasn't caused any problem with my heart. Then I had to take Mum to see her cancer consultant. She couldn't tell if the tamoxifen is working for Mum, so they want a scan doing. We could both do without that.

Friday, 19 August

Mum's scan came through so we went today. Mum finds it painful lying on the table but she was good and they did it quickly. They were able to tell us today that Mum's cancer has shrunk by about 50% so it looks like the medication has it under control. I know this may not last, since becoming intimately involved with cancer, I have read more about it and when there is anything on the news my ears prick up. I know cancer is very canny and once it realises that medication is being used against it, the cancer can change plans and grow differently but for the time being, Mum is doing well. Thank goodness.

Chapter 13
What Pam Did Next

Saturday, 20 August

We went to a Motown Night. I wanted to go but felt very sick getting dressed. It took me ages deciding what to wear and checking I looked OK. I'm happy with people I know but the thought of being in a room with loads of strangers unnerves me. I ask myself: Why does it matter? I have no answer. It was worth it though, as the music was good.

Monday, 22 August

Felt so tired when I woke up. I made it down for breakfast but then had to go up to bed again and Keith didn't see me until teatime. I guess I overdid it on Saturday night.

Sunday, 28 August

I'm in Deal! I came down on the train, Keith wouldn't let me drive and he was right as usual – it would have been too much. Mind you rail travel isn't as relaxing as it's cracked up to be. I had to change twice! I'm staying at Ellie's flat which is at the top of a house on the sea front, six flights up! I'm so happy to be here, there were times when I thought I would never get to do anything like this again. Ellie is at work so I go for walks along the sea front during the day. I've also defrosted her freezer and started packing up her stuff for when she has to move out. She has been given notice as the landlord is selling. She has decided to resign from her job and come home for a while. It will be great to have her around again. I went up to the South Foreland Lighthouse to see her at work. It makes me feel so proud when I see her on site dealing with everything. It is such a beautiful place. I walked along the cliffs and gazed across to look at France.

Wednesday, 31 August

I was very tired when I got home but very proud of myself for having made the journey. I know I'm getting stronger. I had another hospital appointment yesterday. I really didn't want to go, and to make matters worse, they were running late. I go back in three months' time so three months of freedom! Hurray!

Friday, 2 September

I have been to the cemetery today to take some photos. We need to decide what to do about Dad's ashes. I still have them in my wardrobe! I think Dad would understand that we've been distracted and unable to do anything with them. We wanted to take them to Yorkshire which he loved but recently Mum said that Yorkshire is a long way away and her home is here now. I could have kissed her when she said that, it meant so much to know she feels like that about her place. So we've decided to keep Dad in the village close to us. I'm taking photos to show Mum the choices she has. We can bury his ashes in a plot with a small headstone or scatter them in the Peace Meadow and have a plaque.

Tuesday, 6 September

We are in Bristol supposedly enjoying a relaxing time at Stan and Emma's with our grandchildren but I feel so low I want to cry. We stopped at the services on the way down and for tuppence. I could have turned the car around and driven back to Leicester, crawled into bed and wept. What is wrong with me? I know I'm tired, but this is ridiculous.

Saturday, 10 September

We are home luckily, everyone in Bristol seemed to understand what was going on with me. Wish I did! I was horrible to Keith. Ellie rang and talked to me and she made me feel a bit better. I guess I'm going to feel like this sometimes but I don't like not being in control, so it's never going to be easy for me.

Saturday, 17 September

Yet again I have had to have my seroma drained. I think this is the ninth or tenth time they've drained my mastectomy site. The Macmillan nurse was wonderful, I didn't feel it one bit but I do wish it would just settle down now and go away! We also talked about having a reduction of my right breast which is still very large. This means I have to wear a massive prosthetic to match. The prosthetic is silicone and a good shape but it weighs a ton, or at least it feels like it does especially at the end of a long day. I can't wait to take it off in the evening. I have decided I want a reduction ASAP. I will need to speak to my consultant when I see her later this year.

Sunday, 18 September

This time 30 years ago, I was holding a new born Ellie (she was called Eleanor then!). I remember so clearly when they lay her on my chest and I looked into her big eyes; I thought how beautiful she was and how lucky I was. Now she's in Morocco with her boyfriend so I can't see her. I'm crying.

Tuesday, 27 September

I have a new prosthetic; it is lighter than my old one but still heavier than my real breast would be. I sometimes wonder if people can tell it's false when they give me a hug. It is definitely denser than my own breast. If anyone ever ran into me at full pelt, it would floor them!

We celebrated Ellie's birthday with a meal out but Mum was too poorly to come with us, such a shame as she would have loved the food. It seems like she has a chest infection, I've had the doctor out who prescribed antibiotics. We are due to go to Ibiza this week. I am worried about going if Mum is ill but the girls say they have a plan and we must go.

Saturday, 8 October

We made it to Ibiza! I cried on the plane. We have had so many lovely times in Ibiza so when I was really ill and awake in the middle of the night. I would make myself remember the good times as a way to keep away 'bad thoughts'. I promised myself that we would go again and have more wonderful days but deep inside I was never quite sure it would happen. I couldn't stay sentimental for very long on the plane as we were sandwiched in between two large hen parties and all sorts of stuff was kicking off, including girls lifting up their T shirts to reveal naked breasts! What would they have thought if I had done the same, I wonder?

Great news – Emma is pregnant! Their new baby is due on Keith's birthday on May 25!

Mum still hasn't shaken off her cold and her chest doesn't sound right.

Sunday, 23 October

So my hospital visit wasn't a great success. My surgeon, Miss Appleton, says that my seroma, which we call my 'little breast', has organised itself and is no longer liquid but has become dense. My prosthetic is always going to be painful and there is no way that a reconstruction could be done on the left side of my chest. She says that I need another operation to cut away the scar tissue to make my chest flat. She told us that she has only seen this happen to one other woman before me – great, just my luck to have something extra! We are going back in December to see her and a plastic surgeon about my options. I feel pretty miserable, the thought of *having surgery in the new year doesn't fill me with joy but I need something doing as I can't stand this much longer.*

Thursday, 3 November

Mum and I went for lunch together again, first time since before all my treatment. It was nothing special food wise but wonderful to just be doing it again now that both she and I are feeling better. Long may it continue!

Friday, 18 November

My birthday. I wanted it to be low key and it has been lovely. Keith and I went to the Peace Meadow to sprinkle Dad's ashes as Mum had asked us to do. It was lovely and sunny and peaceful down there. I often walk down through the old village and then on past the cemetery and by the Peace Meadow so I can have a chat to Dad when I pass by. I don't really believe in an afterlife but if there is somewhere, then I'm sure Dad is there in his shed telling stories!

Tuesday, 6 December

Mum and I ran a stall at her place on Saturday. We did a Christmas game for the children. Our main customer was Lilli who kept coming back for yet another turn! She also saw Santa, Mum and I watched as she sat on a stool at his feet and talked to him. She looked so small and shy; we have no idea what they talked about. She looked so nervous and kept pulling her dress over her knees then letting it bounce back and then doing it over and over. We both had tears in our eyes watching her.

Wonderful news; Amy has had her baby, a girl called Martha Rose. How lucky I am to share Keith's girls and their husbands and children. We can't wait to go over later to see them all.

Later – we have seen Martha; she is gorgeous but a bit battered as she had quite a hard time. When we got there, she was cold, so the shawl I had made came in useful plus the bootees Mum had sent over. We took a photo to show

Mum who has another head cold so won't see her until she's cleared that.

Saturday, 17 December

We went to see Miss Appleton, my surgeon, again yesterday, we were late going in and I was getting a bit agitated, but the good news is that they are going to sort out my seroma and do the reduction of my right breast at the same time so I will only have one lot of general anaesthetic and one recovery period. Sounds stupid to be celebrating planning an operation but this seems like a victory for me! I have to have it at the main hospital which isn't so good, plus I will have two drains so will be in two nights and recovery time is 5–6 weeks. I can do that.

Tuesday, 20 December

Ellie and all her worldly goods are home! Today we took Mum to see Martha; she held her and chatted to her. Martha stared up at Mum. Children love her probably because she loves children, especially babies. We have a lovely photo of them together.

Thursday, 29 December

Xmas was a real family affair. We were all together, sharing the cooking, the chores, and the children, and enjoying it. Mum came over but went back to her own flat each evening as she was tired by then. It was hard not to think about how I was feeling last year when I was hiding what was going on from everyone but Keith. I thought that this year I would just be able to be ecstatic but I have my anniversary mammogram coming up and I'm scared they will discover something else growing inside me that I've somehow missed. I also fear the unknown – my charmed life seems to have ended. What will life throw at me next?

As I look back over my diary from the end of radiotherapy to the New Year, it is like riding a roller coaster with loads of ups and downs. I have always hated roller coasters.

I remember going to Little Hampton on a day trip and being talked into going on the Wild Mouse ride by Dad. We set off and went down the first slope which was quite tame; I put my head inside his suit jacket and stayed there screaming for the whole ride! Much later, as a mother, I took my daughter on the Dragon Ride at Legoland. She was ten and had to restrain me when I tried to get out at the top of the first run! I like my life to be on an even keel and during these months, it was anything but!

Chapter 14
I've Had My Life

After Christmas had passed, we aimed to get back on with our lives. Mum was delighted when her grandson, Steven, suggested visiting with his family. It was agreed that I would cater at our house so that we would have a bit more space. The children's presents had been held back so that Mum could give them to them herself. When I went to collect Mum, she had started another cold and was worried about passing it on to the children. A lovely time was had by all. The children loved their presents and ate well and Mum lapped it all up. Another 'golden day' on the calendar.

As we crept towards the New Year, Mum's cold worsened and she started to be 'chesty' again. On New Year's Eve, I decided to call in the doctor who immediately prescribed antibiotics. Mum and Dad had stopped celebrating New Year years before, so she wasn't planning to stop up anyway and had an early night instead.

When Dad was a London cabbie and later when he ran his own taxi firm in Immingham, they both worked through the New Year celebrations ferrying punters around. Usually, they had a few minutes together as Big Ben rang out and all the ships in the dock and on the River Humber set off their claxons and then Dad would set out again to pick up the next fare while Mum took phone calls from stranded partygoers. Mum also worked the radio, keeping Dad and his drivers informed. Mum and Dad had always been hard workers. When I was small and at school in London, I can remember my mum having three jobs at a time! She worked part time in a pawnshop, cleaned for a judge and his wife who lived in some 'mansion flats' nearby and also sometimes worked in a pie and mash shop. Dad had never been unemployed, even during difficult times, except for one short period when we moved back to London after a brief stay in Yorkshire. Dad couldn't seem to get any work and was walking a couple of miles every day to a place where they were recruiting drivers on a daily basis. For some reason the person organising this seemed to have taken a dislike to Dad and kept turning him away even when it should have been his turn. After several days of turning up and being denied work, Dad got up early, got my brother, Derek dressed and set off. After being denied work again, he walked into the office and sat Derek on the table and went to walk out. When the man in the office jumped up and asked what Dad was up to, Dad replied that as the man had denied him work again, he would have to feed Derek as Dad had nothing at home for him! The man was obviously shaken and soon found that he did actually need another driver that day and on many occasions after as well!

2016 arrived but Mum's condition worsened. She was having problems breathing and her pulse was racing. The paramedics were called and they decided Mum was in danger of having either a stroke or a heart attack, so we found ourselves in the back of an ambulance again heading for town. Whenever an ambulance passes me in the village now, I wonder if it is an Oak Court resident inside. We were held outside for three hours as A&E was already full to bursting. Mum was amazing chatting to the ambulance crew about how she came to be in Leicester, she even flirted a bit with the driver! I couldn't have been more proud of her, there was no fuss. As I sat there, I thought about the NHS, how had it got to this state that a 90 plus woman would have to lie in an ambulance or on the floor for hours waiting for help? Eventually we made it in through the rubber doors and took our place amongst the ill and distressed. It was ten hours before she was admitted to a ward. I rushed home to have my latest Herceptin injection and then rushed back to check she had settled in. That night I went to bed at 10 p.m. The phone rang at 11.30. I didn't want to answer but made myself, it was Ellie locked out – I had left my key in the inside lock! Phew!

On returning to the hospital the next day, I found that Mum had been moved to a different ward in the middle of the night! Dad always used to say that at least when you're in the hospital you can get a good night's sleep, but this just isn't true anymore. Hospitals have to admit 24/7 which means that other patients are often moved, or even worse, discharged at ungodly hours. I'm absolutely certain that all this can't possibly aid recovery. When I got home from visiting, the newspapers are all full of articles about how our hospitals are overstretched and how elderly people are, through no fault of their own, bed blocking. On local TV I am told that the hospital Mum is in has had its highest number of admissions on record. No wonder it took ten hours to get Mum admitted but what about those behind us, what happened to them? I worry about what it will be like when I'm older, will it be worse? Can it be worse?

Mum didn't seem to be recovering at all so a scan has been completed that shows something in her left lung. It could just be a particle of food inhaled during a good meal or something more sinister – the chest infection is blocking the view. I am thrown into a low mood, believing it could be secondary lung cancer. Now I'm selfishly worrying about how I will cope if this is cancer. I'm already pretty exhausted and sick of hospitals, how could I start again with Mum? I have to put this out of my mind to think about at another time, now I must just get on with it whatever 'it' is.

The next day I open an envelope to find that my operation to remove my seroma and to make my other breast smaller has been scheduled for 30 January. I had almost forgotten about that. Prior to my operation, I have to undergo a mammogram to check that my one breast is cancer-clear. I am very nervous when I approach the clinic. The only good thing is that I only have one breast to squash between those two cold metal plates on that hideous machine! It's done and I set off to visit Mum. I wished I hadn't. Keith was there, the ward was busy and loud. Poor Keith couldn't hear properly and Mum was being awkward, saying the doctor had shouted at her. I was trying to work out what had gone on. Mum was obviously tired so I pulled her curtains and encouraged her to sleep. Keith and I never argue, but we did that day! I went back in the evening only to find that Mum was being moved to a community hospital to rehabilitate her ready to go home even though we still didn't know what was really wrong with her.

Mum's birthday falls in the middle of January, usually I buy her a winter jumper but this year it was hand cream and cake served in the community hospital. Mum was placed in a room on her own which was great because it meant she could get some sleep, but she found it boring not being part of a larger ward. She was always grateful to receive visitors, especially Amy with Martha. If there was a baby in the room, then Mum always had lots of visitors as news would travel fast and the staff would arrive to get a cuddle of the sleeping child! Mum asks about Ellie who has flown to Peru, ready to travel with a friend for a couple of months now that she's free for a while. Mum finds the idea of going to South America pretty alarming, she has never been abroad and never wanted to.

Dad had travelled to Norway but after that he never went abroad again. We didn't travel far but we always had holidays. Before Dad had a car of his own, he would borrow a vehicle and take us off somewhere he had visited as part of his job or during the war. We had an old army surplus tent to start with that. Dad would put it up for us to sleep in. Mum cooked on a primus stove and washed up in a bowl outside the tent door. Gradually we got more sophisticated and Dad bought a tent with two inner sleeping compartments plus a two-ring cooker. That tent went everywhere and we went with it. I have picnicked by the side of Windermere, on the beaches in Cornwall and outside castles in Wales. I have also been washed away in Scotland where all of our belongings ended up hooked on a hedge when they were left high and dry by a torrent that swept through our tent in the middle of the night! It's pretty embarrassing as a teenager to have to go and pick all your underwear off a hedge in front of complete strangers!

On one holiday, in Cornwall, we had some pretty extreme weather. The first week was hot with a heat wave covering the southwest. We basked on the beaches covering ourselves in cheap suntan lotion. No one knew about factors then, and most lotions were probably pretty useless. I can remember having to put camomile lotion on as my legs had burnt all down the front. I also remember Mum putting lotion on Dad who accused her of having sand on her hands, she didn't; he was just burnt bright red, no one thought about covering up. Then the weather was due to change. We heard on the radio (my brother carried it around glued to his ear listening to Radio Caroline or the football results!) that there were going to be gales. It was hard to believe we were in a beautiful harbour where the sun was shining. That night Mum woke up to hear my Uncle Harold shouting, "Hold on to it Dot. Don't let go whatever you do!" She woke everyone up, Dad rushed outside to find Dot hanging on to the centre pole in their little tent while Harold tried to get the guy ropes tied back down; there was a howling wind. They managed it and we all had tea at ours.

The next day we heard that the storm had been bad and had caused damage right along the coast. Dad told us that he'd heard that a boat had broken away from its moorings and ended up miles away on rocks, luckily no one was on board. I threw my brother a sharp glance and he mouthed for me to 'Shut up'. I knew that on the previous day at that picturesque harbour, my cousin and brother, being quite bored, had played a little game. There was a boat tied up by a rope looped over a metal pole on the harbour wall. Derek and Pip had been lifting up the loop and taking turns dropping it back over the pole when one of them missed and the boat began drifting away from the quay. Silently they walked away to find something else to pass the time. Was it the same boat?

The community hospital do their job and Mum is soon up and out of bed and walking to the dining room, so she is ready to be discharged yet again. When I ask what the thing in her left lung is, nobody can tell me. It could be food, it could be that she has COPD. No one seems to think it is cancer, so I breathe a sigh of relief and once more settle her back in to her flat. The staff are happy to see her, they tell me she is the life and soul making them laugh all the time. I'm so glad she has found herself again after the time she spent with us when she hardly smiled at all.

Mum is still smiling a week later when she has fallen over yet again, slid cross the floor on her face and given herself several grazes and a black eye. She was trying to get to the commode, which we started using after she fell over trying to get to the toilet. I arrive three hours before the ambulance and sit on the floor with her. She can't get up once she's down, the staff are not allowed to help her in case she has broken something, so we all wait patiently for the experts. When they arrive, they are, as always, so caring, gentle and good-humoured. They assess Mum and decide to get her into her chair. After a while they assess her again and thankfully decide she doesn't need to go to A&E. I'm so happy for Mum and for me – that's several hours of our lives we've just got back.

Mum may not be in hospital but I'm booked in for my operation, so I get up before 6 a.m. to eat while I can, I can't have anything after 7. I'm always starving as soon as I wake up, woe betide anyone who gets in between me and my breakfast but to get this seroma off and my breast reduced, I'm willing to make the sacrifice. Keith takes me in and then goes off to an appointment. We agree that there is no point him stopping, he can come in later when I'm awake. I give him the car keys and decide to give him my mobile and purse. I am going in via outpatients and not checking in to a ward so am not sure where I can keep my valuables. Keith gives me a big kiss and disappears. I get into my gown and sit in what is just bigger than a broom cupboard. I'm waiting to go down so I keep myself busy reading but can't help noticing that time is passing. Then a young woman arrives to talk to me, she looks pretty nervous, I soon find out why. She's the hospital bed manager and she's here to tell me that they have used my bed for someone else so my operation has been postponed, it is now set for late February. How can I argue or feel angry? Someone needed to be in hospital more than me and is in my bed. I get myself dressed then realise Keith has taken my car keys and what's more, he's taken my car! I also don't have any money and no mobile phone to contact him. I am stranded at the hospital, I think they will probably want this broom cupboard for someone else soon so I'd better make a plan. I don't know his number but then I remember it is probably on my hospital form as next of kin. The hospital, very kindly, let me use their phone and I find £3 in my coat pocket, I go along to the WRVS cafe to see what I can get for £3 – the answer is not much!

I find that I visit Mum everyday now as I feel she isn't really making progress. Each time she has been into the hospital she seems to have emerged diminished in some way. She is unable to recover back to where she was before she was admitted. She is now using the commode all the time, rather than just at night or when she is feeling particularly wobbly. The staff are wonderful and regularly assess whether we need to pay for more hours of support. Thank goodness, we have the money to make these decisions based on nothing but Mum's well-being. It breaks my heart to think of others who have no relatives to care or no money to choose.

Time has flown and I'm back at the hospital for my operation. This time Keith says he will stay until we're sure there is a bed – there is, but instead of being in a room on my own as I was after my mastectomy, or in the plastic surgeon's normal ward, I'm squeezed in somewhere else. I come around after surgery with a crashing headache that lasts a full week. I'm taken up to my ward by a very talkative, kind porter but I really just wish he would stop talking to me and let me suffer. Once on the ward I sleep until Keith visits and even then, I'm finding it hard to be sociable. We take a look down my pyjama top and see two neatly strapped wounds. My right breast looks much smaller and the left-hand side of my chest is completely flat. Hurray! So long seroma!

I am now sporting two drains, one on each side, which cramps my style. They tell me I have to use a bedpan but I'm useless at it. As soon as it is pushed under, I find I can't go and when I force myself, it leaks everywhere, I insist that I can get to the toilet and back with the drains intact and I prove it by doing it when they're busy elsewhere – they decide to leave me to my own devices. That night I'm woken up by the woman opposite me trying to get to the toilet too. She has made it out of bed and is sitting sobbing on the end of her bed. I noticed she is wearing a big, boot-like thing on her foot. I know I can't physically help her in case I break my wounds open but I can't stand to hear her cry so quietly. I try to talk to her without waking the other four people on this side ward. I say encouraging things in a soft voice – I don't know if she can hear me. A nurse arrives and takes over. The next day I realise the woman is a diabetic who has had her toes amputated due to her condition. I soon realise that all of the women in this ward, except me, are diabetics, they are obsessed by food and their sugar readings and can't understand why I'm not. I have to tell them why I'm there, an intruder into their world. I am very glad when I can leave their world to go home, away from the distress and pain they're suffering.

Keith collects me in a wheelchair as I'm too weak to walk to the car in the multi-storey car park. When I get home, I find there is a letter from the hospital saying that they have looked at some X-rays Mum had taken after a trip to A&E and that they now feel she suffered a 'spontaneous wedge fracture'. This means she should not have stood on it, let alone walked. I am quietly very angry, I haven't got the energy to make a fuss as Mum has recovered from that fall now. I find the NHS so confusing. Sometimes they do marvellous work, but, obviously, sometimes it all goes wrong. I am sure that this is not generally down to the staff but to the pressures they are working under. I curse the government for their very, blasé attitude – of course, they all have private health care.

I get on with healing and that's going well. I'm also well on with my Herceptin injections. I have met an array of nurses, I have only once had a repeat! None of them work for the NHS, though they all used to. Most of them worked in chemo wards and found that they needed to get out away from the stress. What a loss. Then I have a hiccup, soon after my operation, the nurse comes to give me my injection and routinely checks my pulse to find there is an erratic beat which has never been there before. Herceptin can damage your heart so I have been having checks, this could be a sign of damage. We decide I will not go ahead and will go to my GP for an ECG instead. I am upset, this is the first time I have ever delayed any treatment. I had chemo on target and also did my radiotherapy in three weeks as planned. I don't want delays, I want to ensure the best outcomes possible and I believe rightly or wrongly staying on time is one way to do this. The ECG is done and it is fine, so I have my injection a week late. I pray it won't make any difference.

Now that I'm healing, I'm on the search for new under-wear and I have to go and exchange my prosthetic for a smaller one. I chose to be a 34DD which I read is quite an average size nowadays. I checked in the shops before I final-ly decided. I wanted to be able to buy my underwear from a high street shop rather than a specialist outlet. I have never been able to buy 'pretty' bras before – by that I mean in nice colours. My size only ever came in white, nude and black and had thick straps and rather a lot of hooks to keep it fas-tened. Now I can have coloured bras and in fact, when I go to change my prosthetic, the volunteer helping me tells me that now I'm smaller I can have a free bra and together we order a purple one! It reminds me of one I was sent by mis-take after my operation. A few days after my operation, I had received a package from a very well-known shop containing a rather daring low cut, underwired purple bra. I found it hard to think who could have sent such an inappropriate gift to a woman who has 'lost' a breast! There was no name on the parcel so I had to ring the company to ask for help. A very quietly spoken man, who I guessed was above retirement age listened to my dilemma. I didn't want to upset the sender if they had really meant me to receive it but if, on the other hand it was an error I didn't want a friend to be charged for something I really couldn't use. He was most understanding and agreed to play amateur sleuth. True to his word he was able to call me back to say the sender would be getting in touch with me. Just a few minutes later a very apologetic friend called to say that having sent me flowers a few days before she had forgotten to change the delivery address when sending the bra which was a sexy gift to herself. She was mortified. We did laugh once she'd got over her initial embarrassment. It may seem strange feeling good about myself when I only have one breast, but I do. I love my new, reduced breast; of course, I wish I had two the same but that's not possible and my new prosthetic is a really good match. Generally, I feel more confident in all my clothes and look forward to buying new ones to complement my new shape. I know many women would not feel like me, but I never really liked my big breasts and don't grieve for them at all.

My happiness with my reduced breast continues but seroma breast is developing again. My breast cavity is yet again filling up with liquid. I have had it drained twice more but it has just replaced itself, so my plastic surgeon and his team are going to drain it then try sticking it together using steroids. After a couple of attempts, it works; I am most relieved.

On Mothers' Day, Ellie, Mum and I go out for lunch together. Three generations of our family. We chat and have fun and I think how lucky I am to have my mum and my daughter here together. Mum insists on having lemon meringue for afters and eats it all. I don't know how she does it. I'm full from the carvery so settle for a cup of tea. Ellie compromises and has both tea and pudding but takes most of the pudding home for later. After the meal we take Mum home then go down to the Peace Meadow – Dad's plaque has gone up and Ellie wants to see it. We talk about Grand-dad and we both have a little cry.

Four days later, Mum is admitted again. She is very breathless and her heart is beating dangerously fast. There is no hanging about; Mum is taken straight onto A&E to the resuscitation unit. Within two hours she is on a ward. I am frightened. I can see Mum's pulse beating in her wrist and it is going too fast for me to count how quick it is. She is in danger of having a heart attack or a stroke. When I leave her to come home to bed, I make sure I kiss her and tell her I love her, I always do, but I do it with determination as I'm worried that her body might give up and she will die while I'm not there. I think she feels the same as I get to the door I turn around and she kisses her fingers to me. She doesn't die, but she starts a pattern that will further exhaust me. Every night, she requests to ring me and when the staff put her on, she shouts and demands that I go and fetch her home. The staff say they're not allowed to say "No" to her, what madness is this?

As this continues, Mum starts to say strange things. She tells me they have shut her out of her flat and I must go around; on another occasion, she insists she's been shut in the frozen food shop and that I have to go and let her out; she sometimes says the ward is shutting, that all the staff are going so she needs collecting. I tell the staff that this is not my mother, she has never been like this before. I think they think she has senile dementia but I keep telling them that until the last few days, all her marbles have been perfectly OK. Her breathing is still poor, so they decide to move her to a respiratory ward in another hospital. When I visit her, she tells me that the ambulance dropped her outside and she found her own way in! I demand to talk to her consultant – I don't, but I talk to someone to explain that I'm worried that she may have a brain tumour. They reassure me that she hasn't but if not, what is wrong with her?

I am having my Herceptin when I receive a call to say that she is going to be discharged. I am incredulous. I ask to speak to the discharge nurse. I can't leave the house for two hours once I've had Herceptin; otherwise, I would drive up there and shout at someone! The discharge nurse will ring me. I wait all day rehearsing my speech – my mum can't come out, she hasn't walked for seven days, she needs preparing. I get the phone call; I'm told there was a misunderstanding, Mum isn't being discharged at all. I sob with relief and frustration.

When I go in to see Mum twice a day, I notice she is getting more and more tired. I encourage her to sleep while I'm there, but just as she is nodding off, she jolts herself awake. It is almost as if she can't allow herself to sleep. The nurses have started getting her ready for discharge, I can't believe it will happen, but it does. She is back at her flat, we can't take her to our house as all her aids are at her flat. She can't manage without her commode, her bedsides, her perching chairs and the help of the staff. Our bed settee downstairs is too low for her and our stairs are too steep for her to sleep up there. We have no choice. Miraculously, once home, her GP prescribes some sleeping tablets and she settles again.

Keith and I agree that we will have to cancel our short break in Ibiza but Ellie and Amy have put together a rota to prove that we can go away and Mum will be well looked after. They have worked it out so that someone will visit every day, plus the staff are on duty 24/7 – they convince us to have a few days away. We get back at 1 a.m. in the morning and receive a call at 7.50 saying Mum is to be readmitted. I know something more is wrong with her, but she has been scanned for everything. Several days after she was admitted we arrive for evening visiting to find her bed empty. We are told she has gone for a scan; she returns looking dreadful. I just hold her hand until she falls asleep. I demand to see her consultant the next day – I don't want Mum to go through any more.

When I arrive, the consultant is waiting for me. Very kindly, I'm told Mum has secondary liver cancer. The plan now is to fast-track her to a care home. I agree that Keith and I will visit the ones they suggest, ones that cater for end-of-life. Mum could live six months or die much sooner, we don't know. I ask that they cease taking blood tests, doing scans etc. as these cannot help her now. For them to agree, Mum must be told she has liver cancer and must be asked if she wants treatment or just making comfortable. I remember what Mum said over two years ago. She said, "I've had my life." Well, now she'd had quite a lot more life but I was sure she wouldn't want treatment or to be resuscitated. I asked the consultant if we could tell her together. This turns out to be quite difficult. It is not the consultant who will come with me to tell Mum, but a less experienced member of the team. I'm not sure how many times she has done this before, but I guess not many if any. First the doctor must check if Mum is rational enough to make the decision. She does this by asking Mum some factual questions about which day it is and where we are. I have my fingers crossed; on some days Mum is so confused she could get these wrong and I want to do this now while I'm ready. Mum responds well and then we try to tell her. I thought the doctor would lead but she is obviously hesitant, so I tell Mum that another cancer has been found in her body. She is surprised but asks about treatment. I wait for the doctor to add to the conversation, she remains silent so I tell Mum that no treatment will cure her and that if she stays in hospital, she will have to have regular blood tests. I asked what she would like to do, she had to choose between staying in the hospital or move somewhere else where she can be pain-free and we can all visit her when she wants us to. It was hard, but once Mum realised that all the treatment the hospital could offer wouldn't make her better, she made the decision that she just wanted to be made comfortable and pain-free. The doctor left, Mum and I ate some early strawberries I had taken and then I put some hand cream on her hands and massaged it in for her. Mum said, "I don't think I'll go out tomorrow." She fell asleep and I left. It was the last time I was to see her awake.

The next day as we were visiting a nursing home, the hospital phoned to say her organs were shutting down and that I should return. As Mum was already in a side room I could stay over and we could visit at any time. It wasn't the best of circumstances but the staff were wonderful, doing their best for Mum and for me. I slept there on a chair for two nights just staying close to her. Sometimes Ellie stayed too and other family members visited, but she didn't wake up. Finally, on 19 May, Keith sent me home to shower, I fell asleep on the bed and Ellie woke me up to say that nanny had died at 9:50 am Keith told me later that he had been talking to Mum telling her that Ellie and I were fine and that he would look after us and that there was no need for her to worry. She waited a few minutes, sighed and died. It was as if she wanted to wait until we'd stopped fussing or perhaps, she didn't want to give us the final pain of seeing her die. I didn't mind not being there; I had done my best for Mum and I knew she realised that. I truly believe that it is what you do in life, how you show your love in the way you live and behave that counts far more than those last few hours of handholding.

Chapter 15
Legacies

My mum and dad were very different people. As my dad aged, he spent a lot of his time looking back into the past and telling stories of good times. My mum, on the other hand, liked to live 'in the moment', neither looking backward nor forwards, like a blindfolded Janus. I funnily enough am similar to neither, but take from both, I like to look forward and plan but I like to learn from the past and believe this combination makes me strong.

I always like to think that all experiences, good or bad, leave a lasting legacy that can be positive. This is the way I have tried to live my life, looking back on things that have happened, often finding that in retrospect things that were hard or stressful at the time are funny and make good stories to tell to others. If they're not funny, using them to learn something that can be applied to new situations.

One of the positive legacies of this difficult time in my life was financial. Mum and Dad had savings. They had run a small business together; a taxi firm. Dad drove and Mum handled the calls and the customers. It was pretty successful; Immingham is a large port with several docks. People need to get into Grimsby which is nine miles away with only a half hourly bus service. Dad worked long hours when others would have been at home watching T.V. He didn't mind getting up early, he was used to it after driving lorries long-distance. Mum matched him, answering the phone from home and relaying jobs to Dad and the other drivers while keeping the house ticking over and meals on the table. Derek and I kept encouraging them to spend their money, telling them we didn't need or want it. As they got older, it became more difficult for them to do that as they didn't get to the shops much. Ironically, Dad refused to use taxis and Mum got travelsick on the bus!

When Dad died, I sorted out Mum's finances and it was clear they had enough money for her to pay the rent for her flat at Oak Court, plus pay for the care she needed which was on an upward trajectory. I was able to reassure her that her money would keep her comfortable for as long as she lived. At that time, I believed she could reach 100 or even more. The house had been sold but it would have broken Dad's heart to know how little it went for. He had always kept up with repairs and decorating but, of course, it was old-fashioned and even a new kitchen and a slightly older conservatory didn't give the ex-council house curb appeal! Nevertheless, it all went in the coffers. So when Mum died, the estate came to Derek and me. I had already decided that this money would go into savings, ready for the girls to have if anything happened to me. Now I realised that I could just give it to them, why wait?

Each of the girls has earmarked theirs for something different, but each time any of them spends or plans to spend or just checks their savings, they thank Mum and Dad. I did keep back a little money so that we could all go on a family holiday. Holidays were really important to my parents and some of the photos I treasure most, are of holidays in Yorkshire, Cornwall, Wales, the Lake District and Scotland. I know that when I was young, very few of my contemporaries had seen as much of the UK as me. We were lucky to always have access to a car and Dad to drive us. I'm not sure what Mum and Dad would have thought of Disneyland Paris but that's where we went. On our wall at home we have a fantastic photo of the whole family wearing Mickey and Minnie ears posing with Pluto the cartoon dog. The kids have been running around chasing him and climbing on his lap, kissing his nose and stroking his back. Us adults have all gate crashed the photo and are squeezed in together. I look at it most days and smile and am so thankful we had this wonderful time together. Who knows what is in the future but this memory is here for ever?

My daughter has continued Mum and Dad's love of holidays in their beloved caravan. She has taken it a stage further by travelling through the outback of Australia in a small van with a bed in the back! She told me that when she was driving the thousands of miles, she covered she thought of Mum and Dad. She remembered all the times they had taken her away for weekends and she had helped Granddad fetch the water and take the rubbish out. She always slept in a cosy caravan surrounded by their love. She remembered when she managed to give them both nits on one memorable weekend in Nottinghamshire. She was 'loving the van' in Oz and thought Granddad would have loved it too.

As far as the cancer goes, I have heard people say many times that having a scary illness or a near death experience helped them to get things into perspective and made them prioritise the important things like family. I don't feel that I needed cancer to do that; I already valued my family above everything and knew how lucky I was to share being a grandparent with Keith. However, it has brought my daughter and me closer in some ways. We went through some difficult times as she was growing up, we loved each other but weren't too sure how to show it sometimes. I was never sure how much advice Ellie wanted or needed. For her part she shared the bad bits but forgot to share the good. In amongst all this cancer stuff and dealing with nanny being ill, we learned to share the good and bad. I learnt that my daughter is stronger than I thought and that I don't have to act as a shield all the time or always be strong. I think she learned just how much I loved her and some of the funny ways I have of showing that love.

I have some physical legacies that are not as positive. The nerves in my feet were damaged by the chemo and so I have this continuous feeling of wearing wrinkled socks even when I'm barefoot. Sometimes, this turns into actual pain. I don't let it stop me dancing, walking, and recently I have taken up running. My fingernails concern me more. Two years on from the end of chemo, the nails are still weak and split and tear. I have a regime of using hand cream several times a week. I can often be seen siting on the settee wearing linen gloves. Usually when this happens, Keith takes the mickey by doing a Marcel Marceau type mime at which I can't help but laugh. Now and again, I wear nail varnish but only on special occasions because it seems that taking it off weakens my nails. Sounds dreadful, doesn't it, but it's a small price to pay for being alive. My eyebrows are thin and patchy, so most days, unless I'm sure I'm not going out, I draw them on and colour them in. Luckily there are lots of products on the market for doing this. I've also changed the way I apply my eye make up to disguise the fact that my eyelashes are short and stubby and unruly, some of them have grown back pointing sideways

My hair has never thickened up, but I love it short. I always wanted short hair, but long was the trend in the 60s and 70s and then I wasn't brave enough to go really short. Now I go to a barber's where the girls cut it in about ten minutes for me. I love the fact that there's no fuss – I don't want a head massage; I just want a trim. I don't have to book in advance, I'm home again in 15 minutes! It also costs about a third of what I used to pay! I've always worn big earrings and have a large collection which continues to grow. Now that I have less hair, you can see my earrings much better. I also wear bigger glasses to make up for the hair loss.

Chemo has left me with other physical leftovers that I could do without. The mastectomy and, in particular, having my lymph nodes removed have left we with some numb places where the nerves were cut through to get access to the nodes. I still can't feel anything under my left arm and have to put my deodorant on by sight only. My fingertips are strangely sensitive so I have to be careful in hot water or when making snowballs. There are many things I struggle to open now in the kitchen and in my make-up bag, I can often be found prising open a lid with a knife or with my teeth! I have a couple of patches of skin on my face that don't act like the rest and are often dry and wrinkled. I thought these things would make me less confident but they don't, this is still me.

Having a prosthetic can be a real pain; physically it is heavier than a normal breast and presses down onto my chest, it is impossible to make anything that really feels like flesh. Flesh is soft and accommodating whereas a prosthetic isn't. I notice this most when with my grandchildren. I'm aware that on my left side I'm not a warm, cuddly nanny. I expect that one day one of them, when sitting on my lap having a snuggle, will notice it and ask me why. I also notice it when greeting friends who give me a quick hug, I wonder, *can they feel the solidness of it?* It also makes getting changed in public difficult. I am ashamed that I once used it to my advantage in Italy. It was our first full holiday after all our trauma. Keith and I were enjoying a wonderful break staying in Sorrento. We had taken a boat over to Capri and had found our way to a small beach. It was pretty empty, just a few families and us. I had my costume on ready and was soon swimming in the little cove, heaven! Then it was time to eat and I ran into a problem. I had forgotten that I would need to not only take off my costume in public, but before I could put my bra on, I would need to dry and transfer my prosthetic to my bra. I had no idea how to manage this without giving those on the beach an eyeful. To be honest, I wasn't too bothered about the adults, but I didn't want to traumatise any small children! I decided to use the restaurant toilets even though there were signs up saying 'No changing'. I crept over to the door in my costume and towel, with my clothes in a bag – just as I was entering, I heard a loud shout in Italian, it was obvious I'd been spotted. A woman was shouting and gesticulating at me, I don't speak Italian, so I did the first thing that came into my head; I pulled down my costume to reveal my flat, scarred chest! Immediately, I was allowed in the cubicle. We had to buy drinks and food afterwards as I felt so ashamed of myself for using my scar in this way! Now I have a spare prosthetic that stays in my swimwear.

Sometimes I'm afraid. I was once asked to buy a T-shirt in aid of a breast cancer charity. It more or less said 'been there got the T shirt'. However, there was more to it; it also said that I wasn't afraid now that I was cancer free. I couldn't buy it because I am afraid sometimes when I let myself think. I know lots of people who have had breast cancer and survived three, five, ten years or more. That should make me brave, but I worry that I'm going to be the one who doesn't survive. Having the treatment I had has given me the best chance of not getting cancer again, but it isn't infallible and I have to learn to live with that. Most days, I just get on with enjoying my life, doing the things I need to do, but sometimes fear gets in the way. The anniversaries of my finding the lump and my diagnosis are both difficult, attending my annual mammogram keeps me awake for days before and after. Friends have died of different cancers and I find it hard to hear as I know it will lower my mood and my ability to get on with life, I have been known to take to my bed for a weekend to conserve energy, ready to face the world again. When I'm afraid about cancer, I miss my parents more – as you can imagine, there are times when I can be a real wet blanket but it passes.

Cancer has made me not trust my instincts about my body. This fear lingers and reappears unavoidably at the most inconvenient times. Just as I'm having a 'whale of a time', I start to wonder if this is going to be snatched away. When I develop a cough or some other small, meaningless ailment as we all do, I find I'm looking cancer up on the internet to decide whether this is secondary cancer in its infancy. I think that every single day I think about having had cancer and wonder if it is going to return. I have spoken with other cancer survivors and I think I am not alone. I can't do anything about this, so I have learnt to do something with it. When I get the feeling that bad things are out to get me, I try to enjoy the moment I'm in even more. I think I already had a good idea of what to value. I don't chase money or status or tick off some list of experiences; mainly, I enjoy what I do and what I have, relationships, friendships and, at the top of the list, family. Cancer hasn't changed that.

I guess one of the legacies of having cancer is that I've learnt more about the people who surround me. I've learnt how strong the girls can be and how positive they are. I've learnt that Keith is amazing and more caring than I imagined anyone could be. He has hidden strengths that saw us through some very difficult days and I know how much he loves me, enough to put up with everything I said and did. I've also learnt that some people can't deal with cancer for all sorts of reasons. Friends reacted in different ways. Some initially sent bouquets and cards and then never contacted us again, while others quietly accepted our rules for communicating and visiting and were always there when I was ready to come out and face the world, whatever state I was in. I'm really grateful to everyone who treated me like a real person and not just a cancer sufferer, who talked about real things, who even shared their bad stuff because it gave me the chance to support them rather than feeling I was the one who needed all the help.

When my mum was alive, I was so focused on her I don't believe I grieved fully for my dad. Initially after Mum died, I was so exhausted that all I felt was emptiness plus a sense of relief that it had all happened quickly at the end so she didn't suffer and I could cope and be there for her. Now that I have regained my strength, I find that I am allowing myself to think of them more and that is the way I choose to grieve. This book is my legacy. I wanted to write it as not only a witness to this part of my life, but also as a tribute to my parents who were very ordinary people in many ways but whose lives enriched this world and have left a lasting impression which I hope will be remembered by my family in years to come. They didn't do anything extraordinary, but the sum total of all their actions made a difference to me and I hope I have, and can continue to, make a difference for others.

Five days after my mum died, our fourth grandchild Freya Rebecca was born in Bristol. Keith and I were there to welcome her to our family. My mum knew she was due but couldn't wait, she would have loved her I'm sure. Love goes on.